A MUSICAL COLLECTION
CIRQUE DU SOLEIL®

Photos: Al Seib, Camirand, Richard Termine Costumes: Dominique Lemieux © 2003, 2007 Cirque du Soleil Inc.

Alfred
Alfred Publishing Co., Inc.
16320 Roscoe Blvd., Suite 100
P.O. Box 10003
Van Nuys, CA 91410-0003
alfred.com

Copyright © MMVIII by Alfred Publishing Co., Inc.
All rights reserved. Printed in USA.

ISBN-10: 0-7390-5126-1
ISBN-13: 978-0-7390-5126-9

Photos: Camirand, Thomas Muscionico, Al Seib, Richard Termine Costumes: François Barbeau, Dominique Lemieux, Thierry Mugler © 1999, 2002, 2005, 2007 Cirque du Soleil Inc.

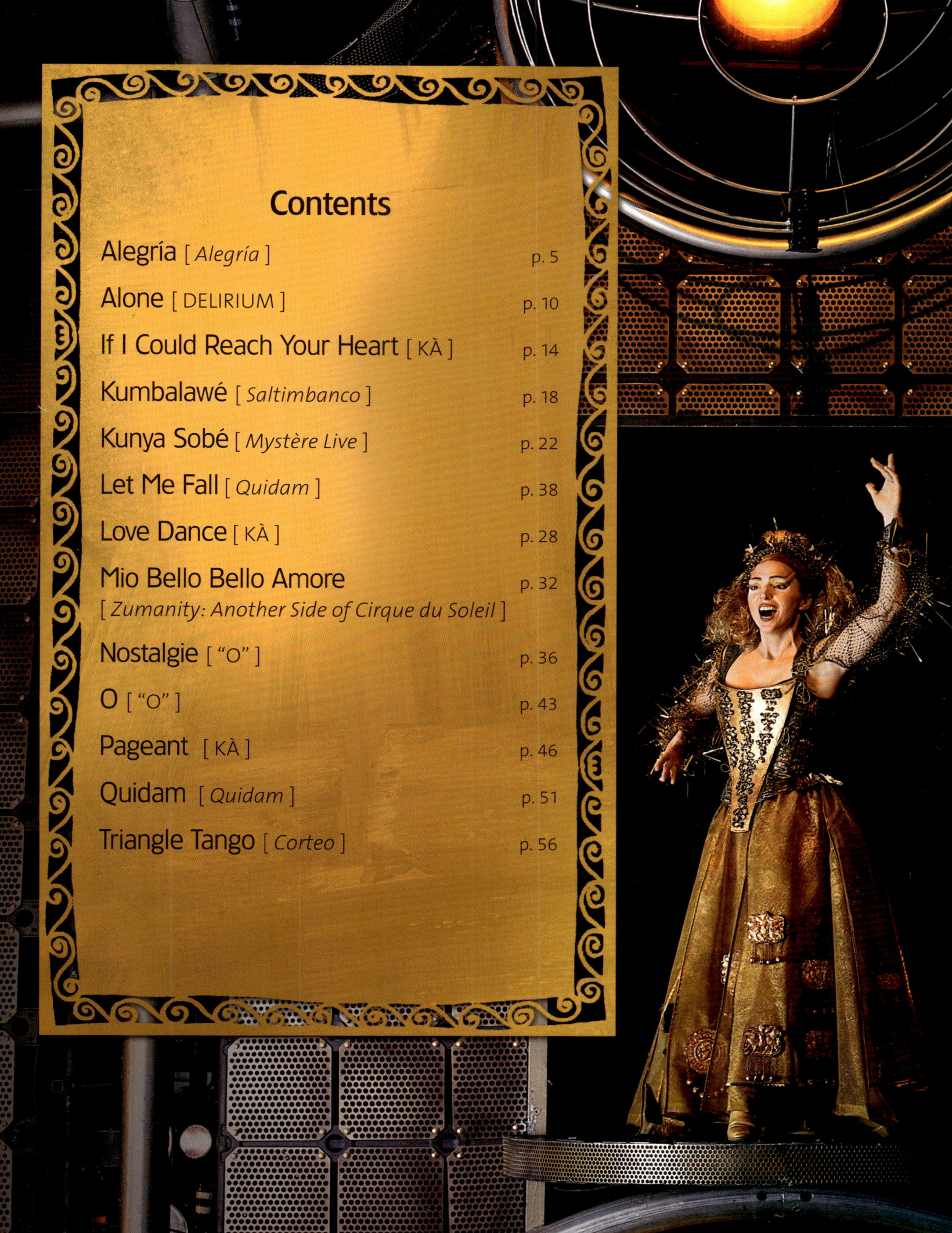

Contents

Alegría [*Alegría*] — p. 5

Alone [DELIRIUM] — p. 10

If I Could Reach Your Heart [KÀ] — p. 14

Kumbalawé [*Saltimbanco*] — p. 18

Kunya Sobé [*Mystère Live*] — p. 22

Let Me Fall [*Quidam*] — p. 38

Love Dance [KÀ] — p. 28

Mio Bello Bello Amore
[*Zumanity: Another Side of Cirque du Soleil*] — p. 32

Nostalgie ["O"] — p. 36

O ["O"] — p. 43

Pageant [KÀ] — p. 46

Quidam [*Quidam*] — p. 51

Triangle Tango [*Corteo*] — p. 56

Photos: Olivier Samson Arcand, Veronique Vial Costumes: Eiko Ishioka, Marie-Chantale Vaillancourt © 2002, 2007 Cirque du Soleil Inc.

ALEGRÍA
(from "Alegría")

Music by René Dupéré
Lyrics by Franco Dragone, Manuel Tadros
and Claude Amesse
Arranged by Dan Coates

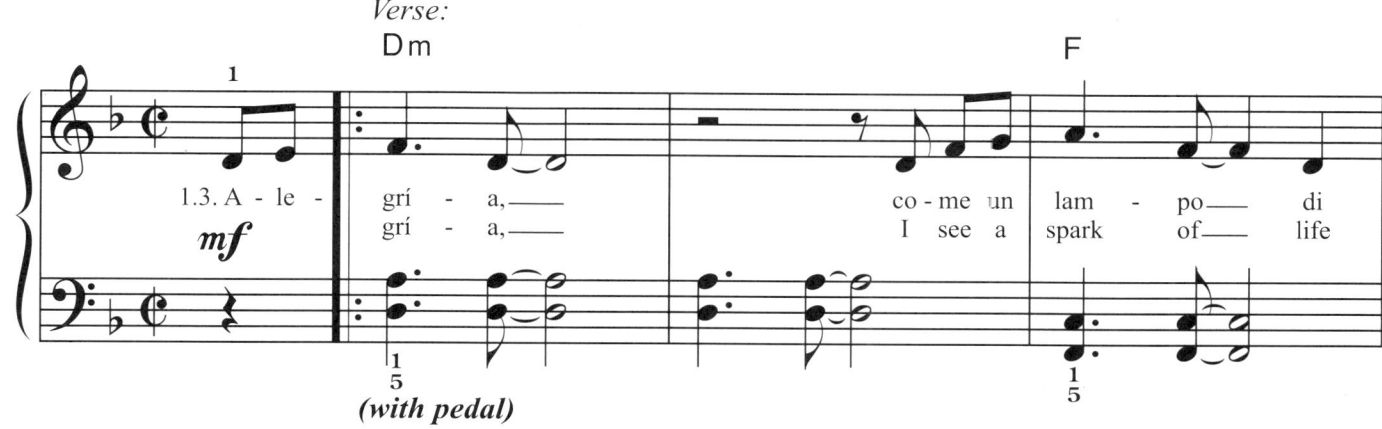
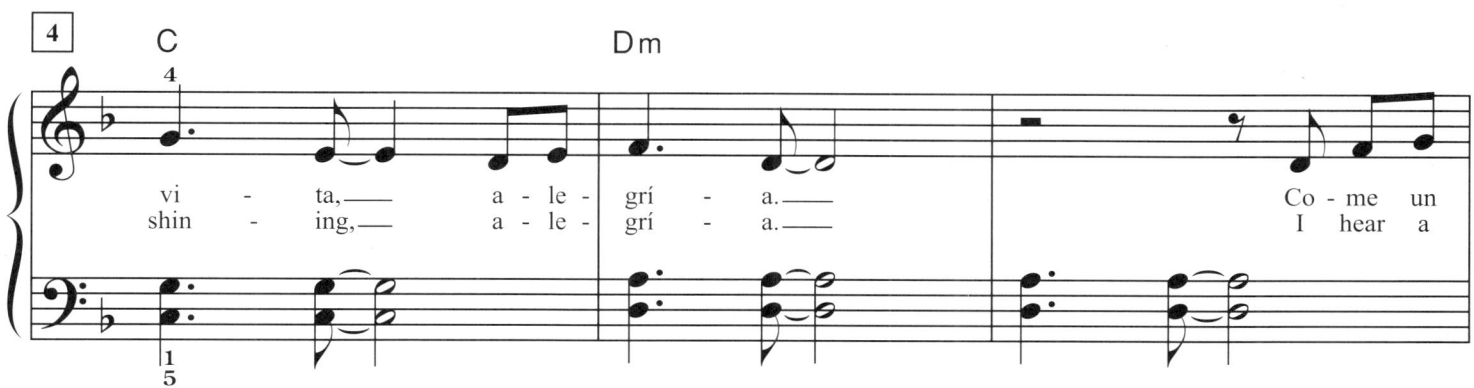

© 1994 CRÉATIONS MÉANDRES INC.
All Rights Reserved

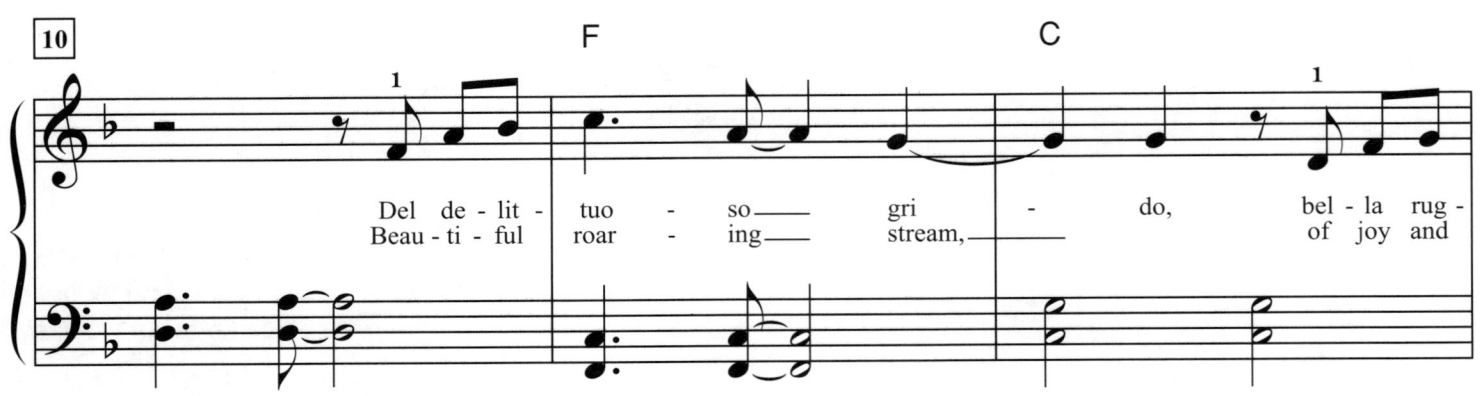
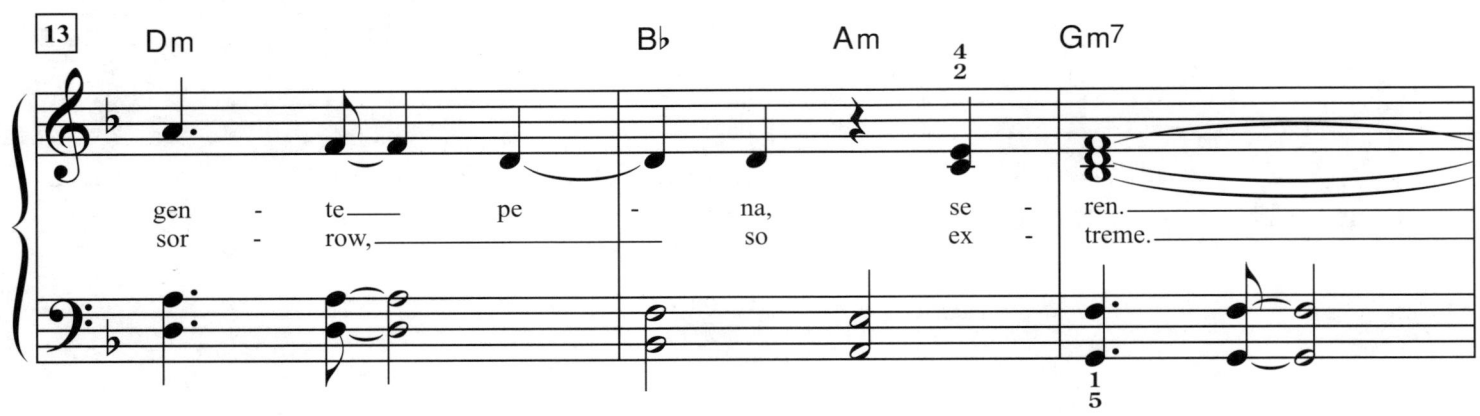

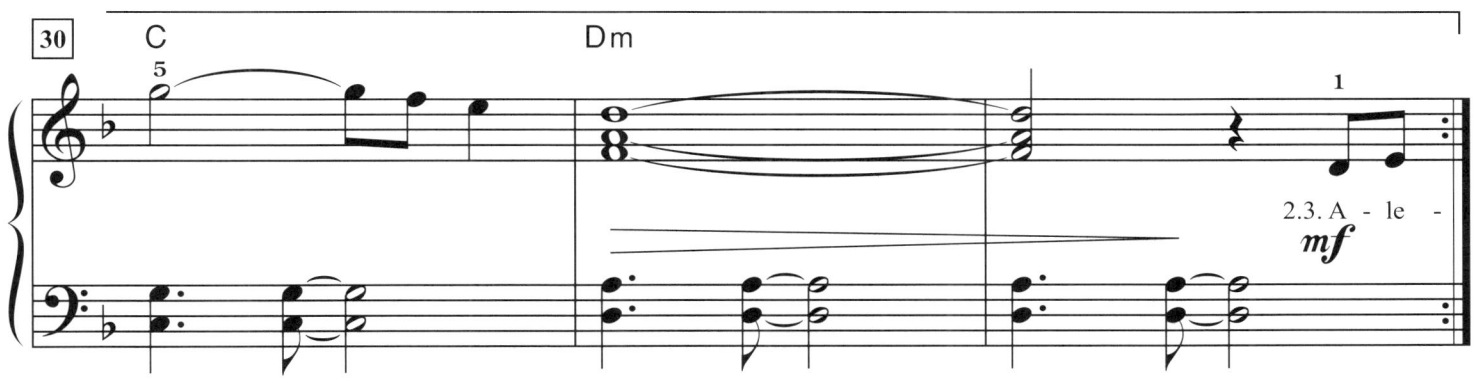

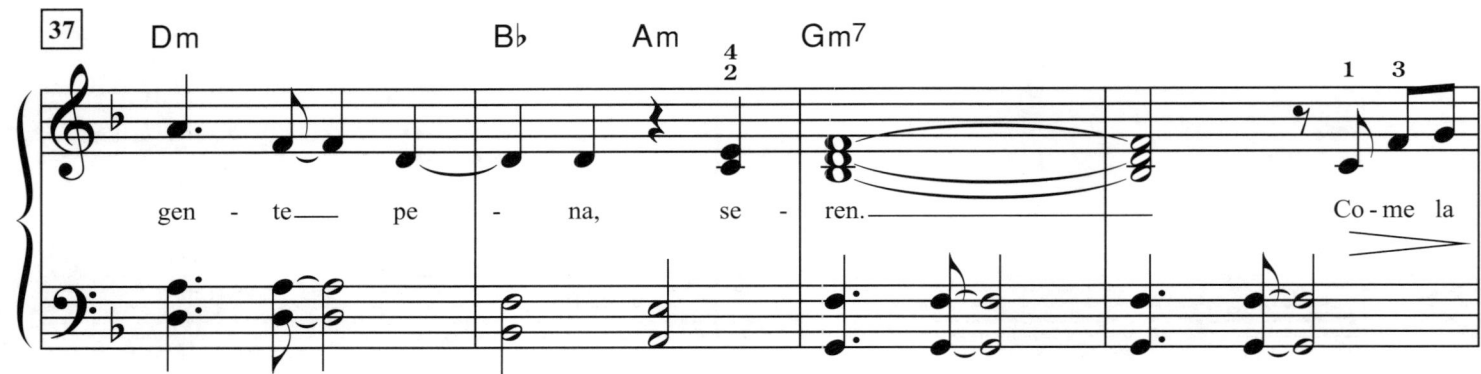
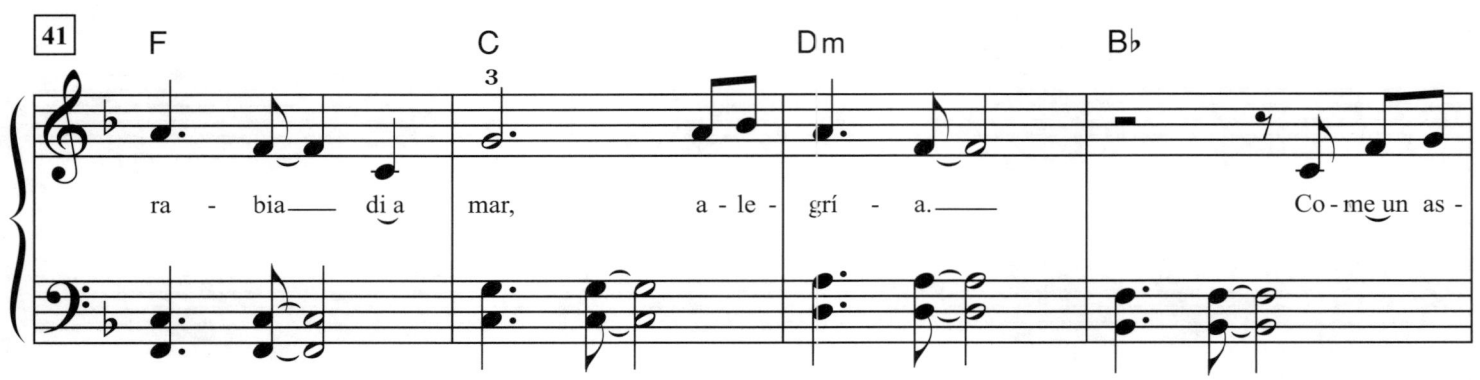
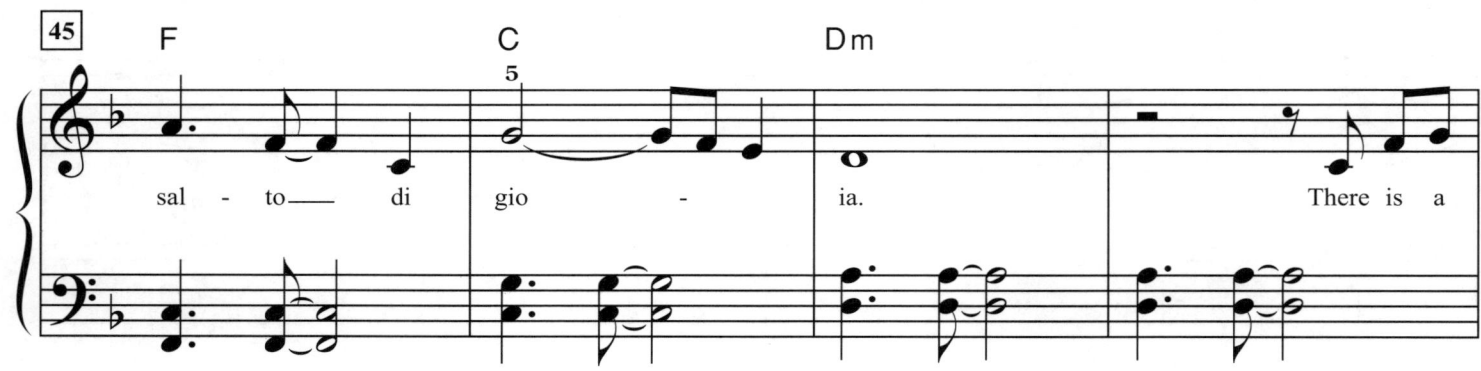
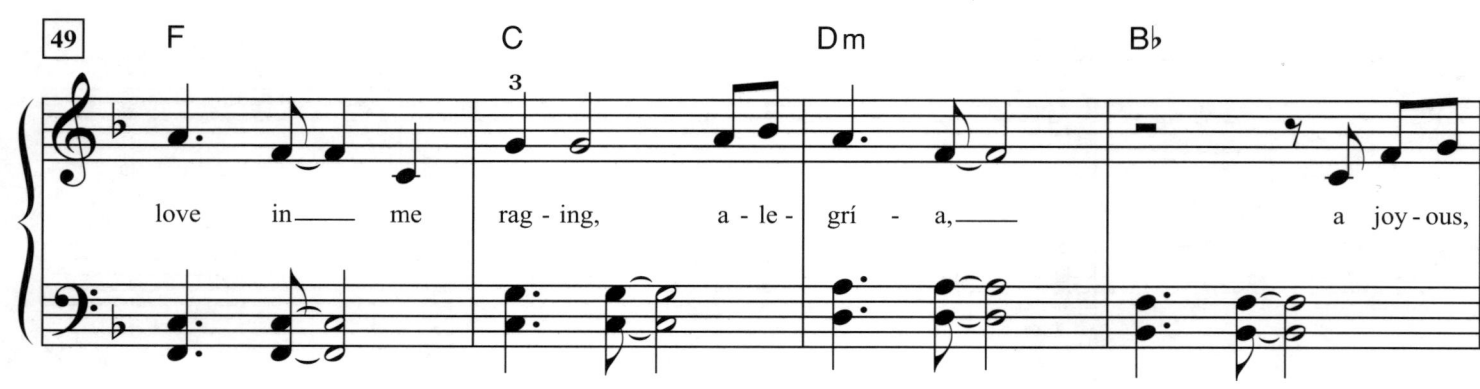

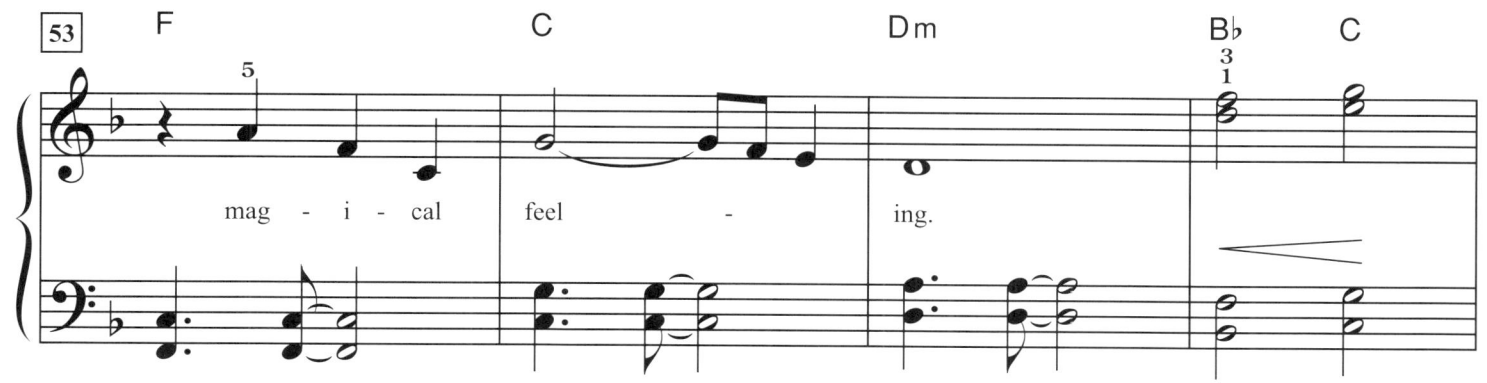
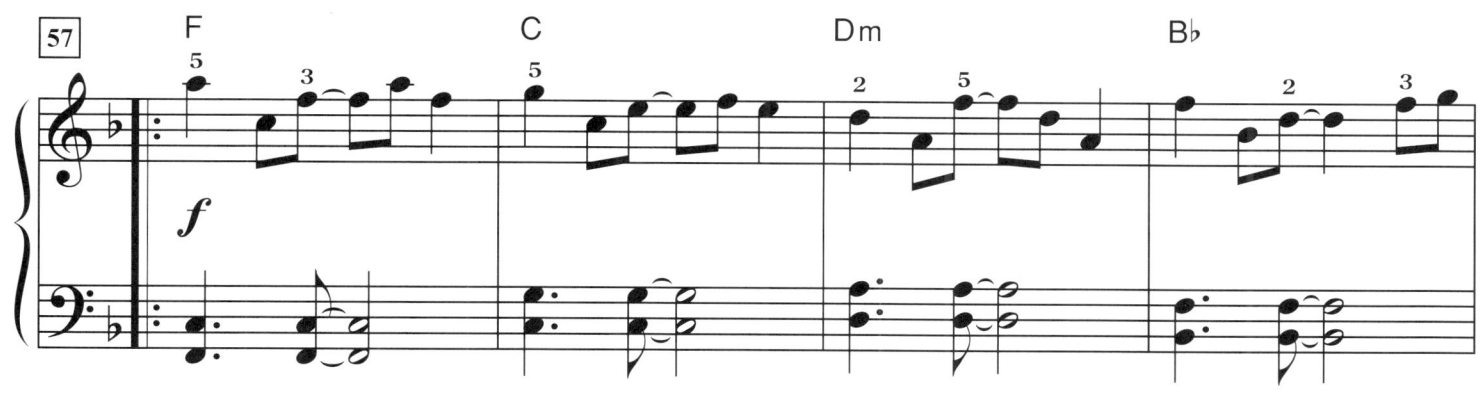

ALONE
(from "DELIRIUM")

Music by René Dupéré
Lyrics by Robert Dillon and Manuel Tadros
Arranged by Dan Coates

© 2006 CRÉATIONS MÉANDRES INC.
All Rights Reserved

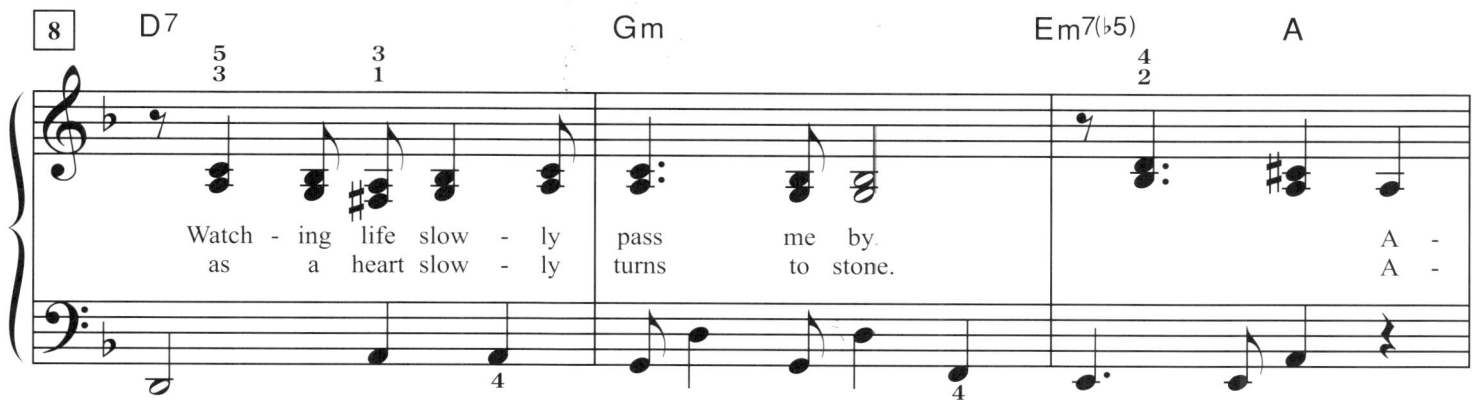
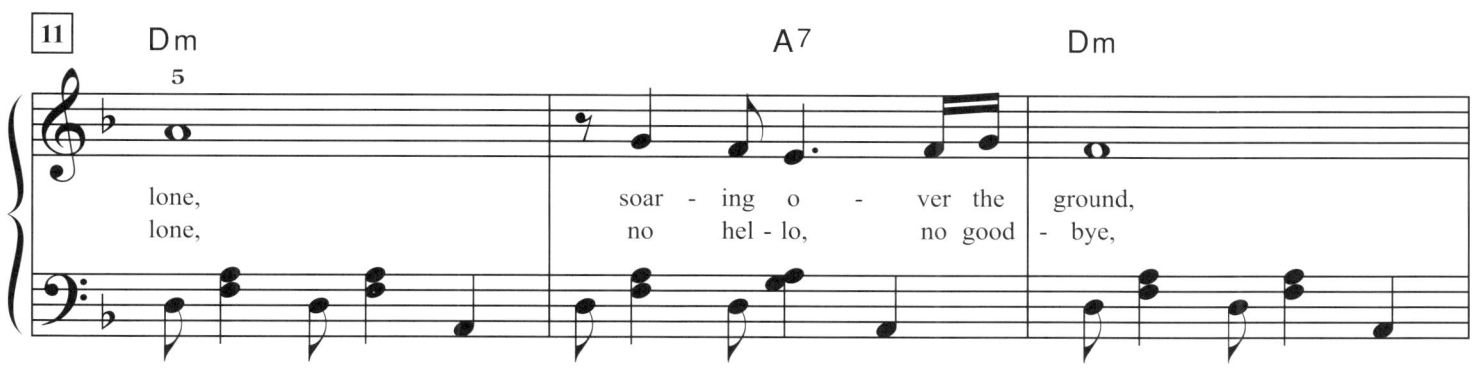

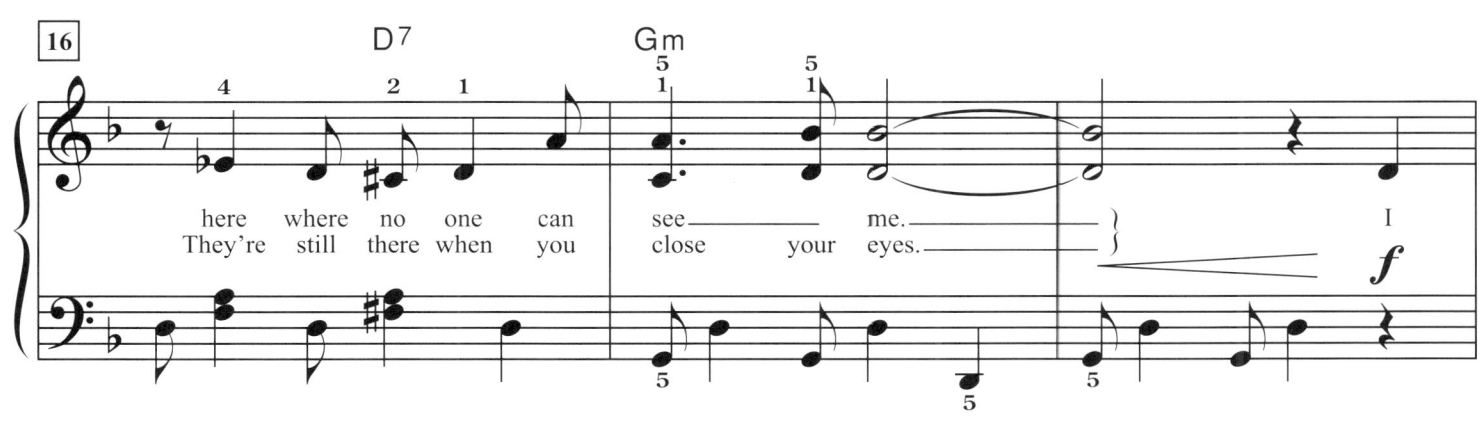

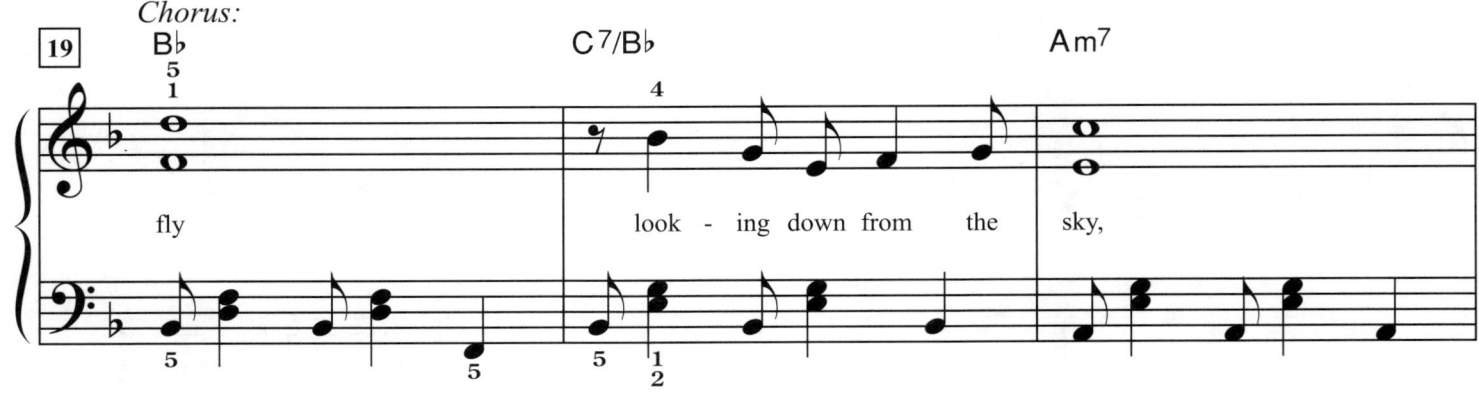
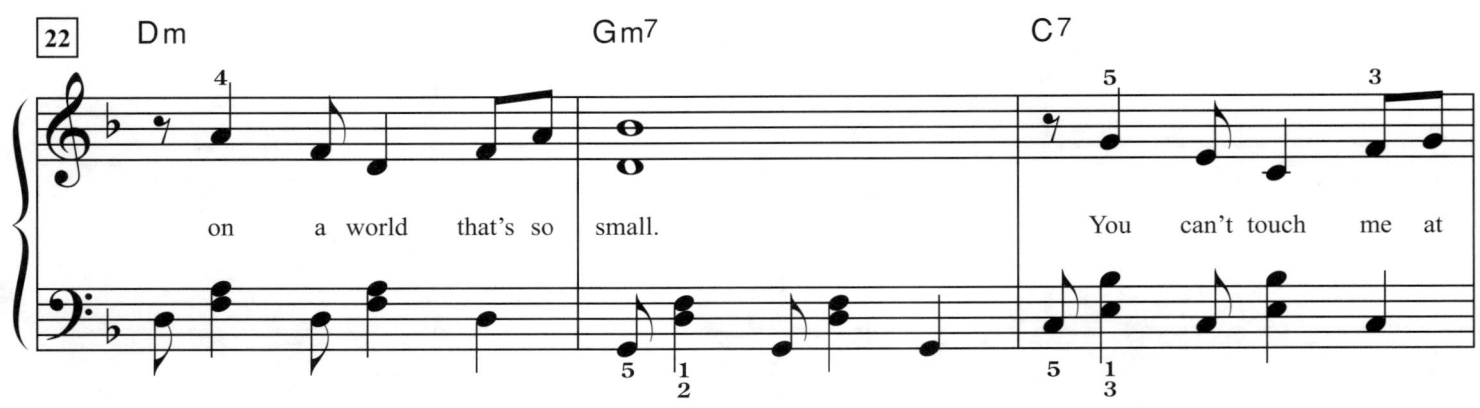
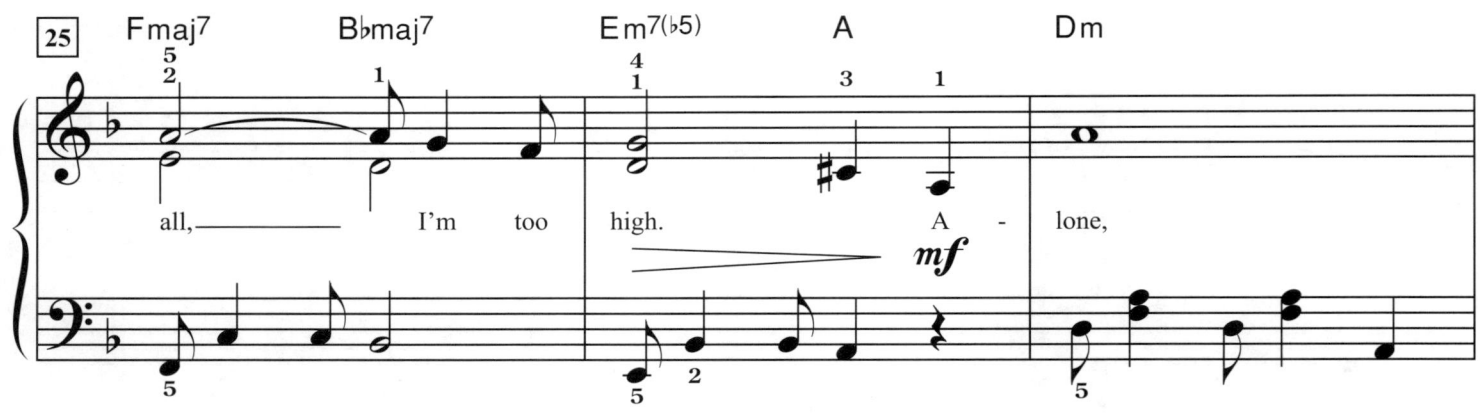
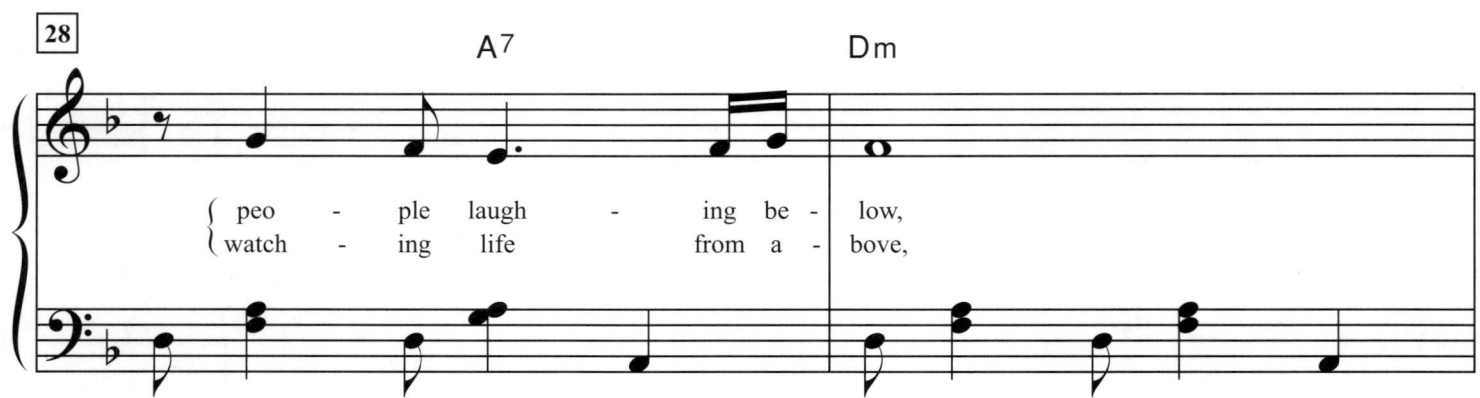

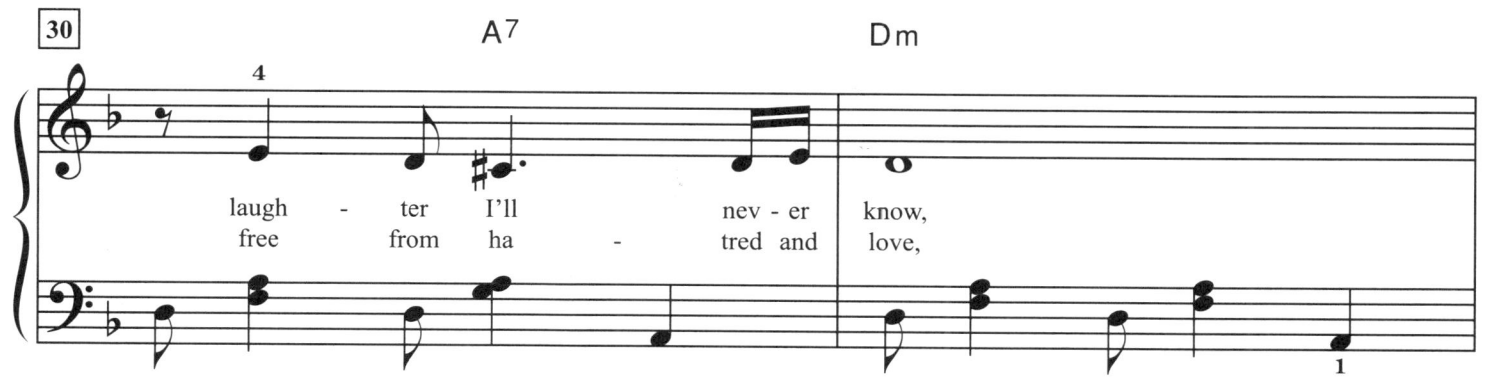
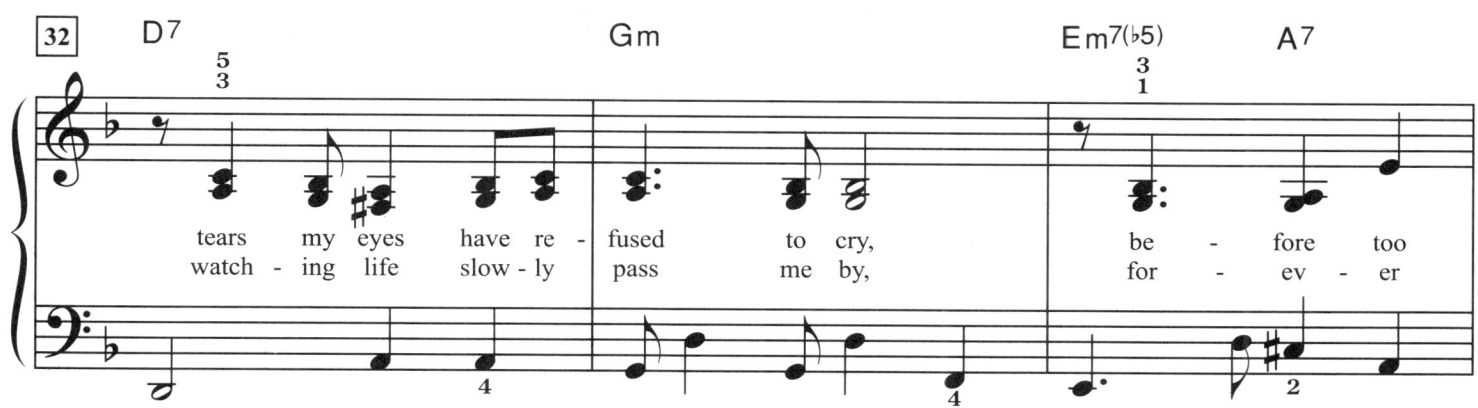
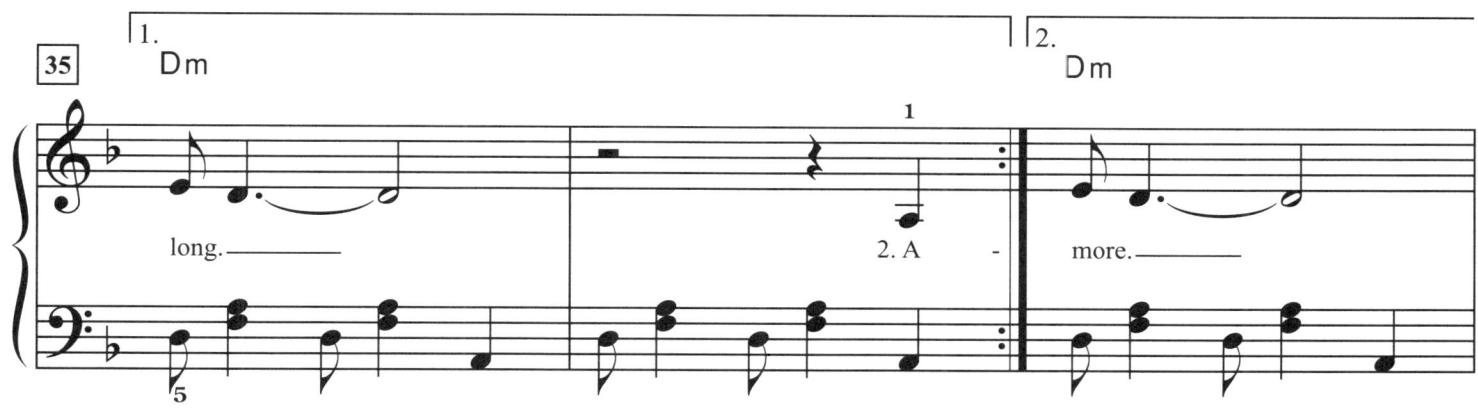

IF I COULD REACH YOUR HEART
(from "KÀ")

Composed by René Dupéré
Lyrics by Ella
Arranged by Dan Coates

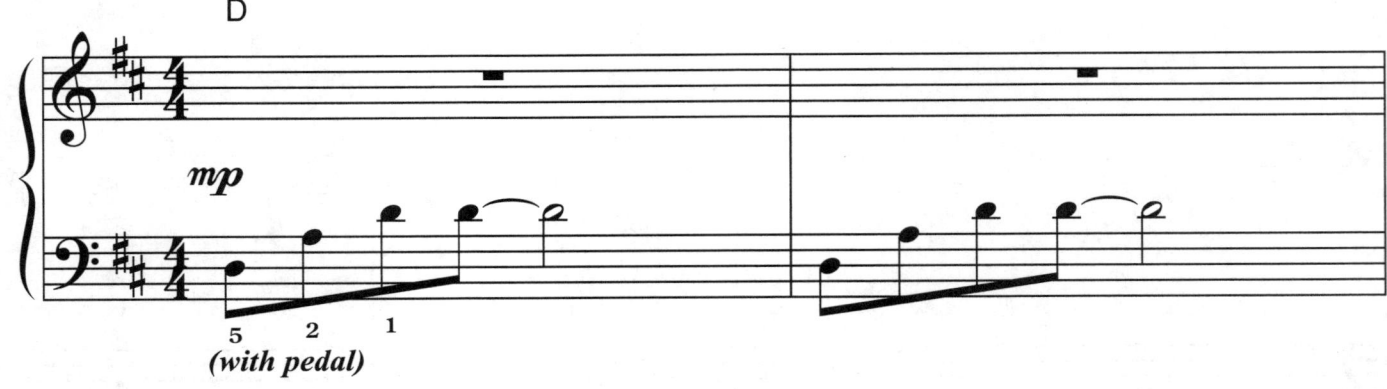

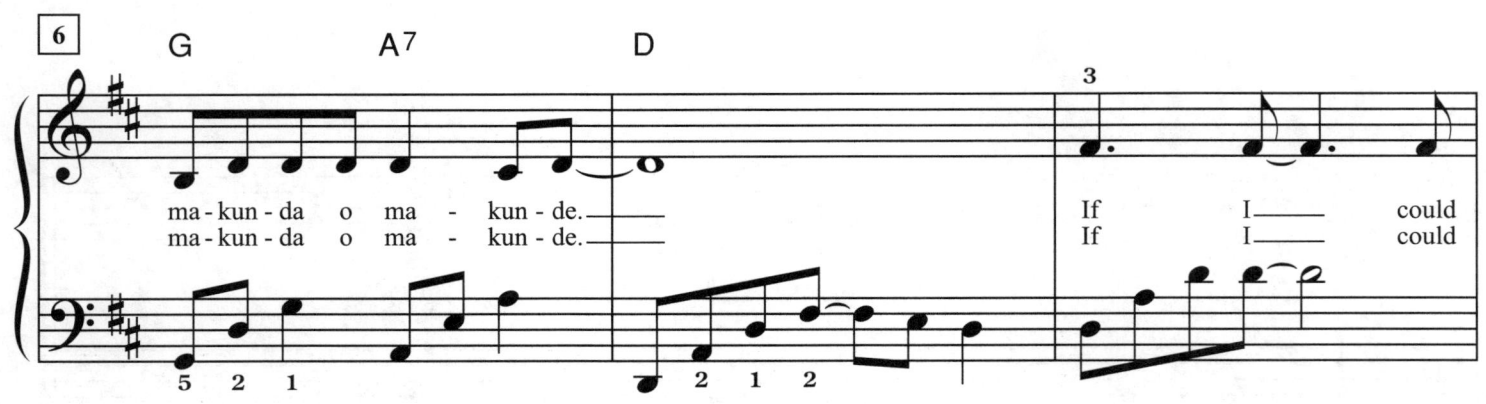

© 2005 CRÉATIONS MÉANDRES INC.
All Rights Reserved

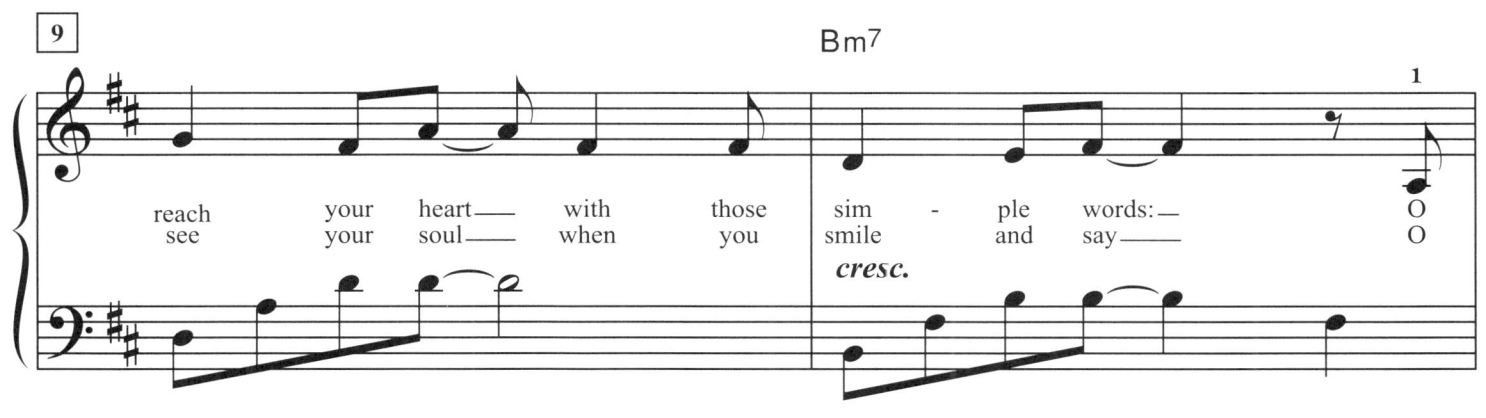
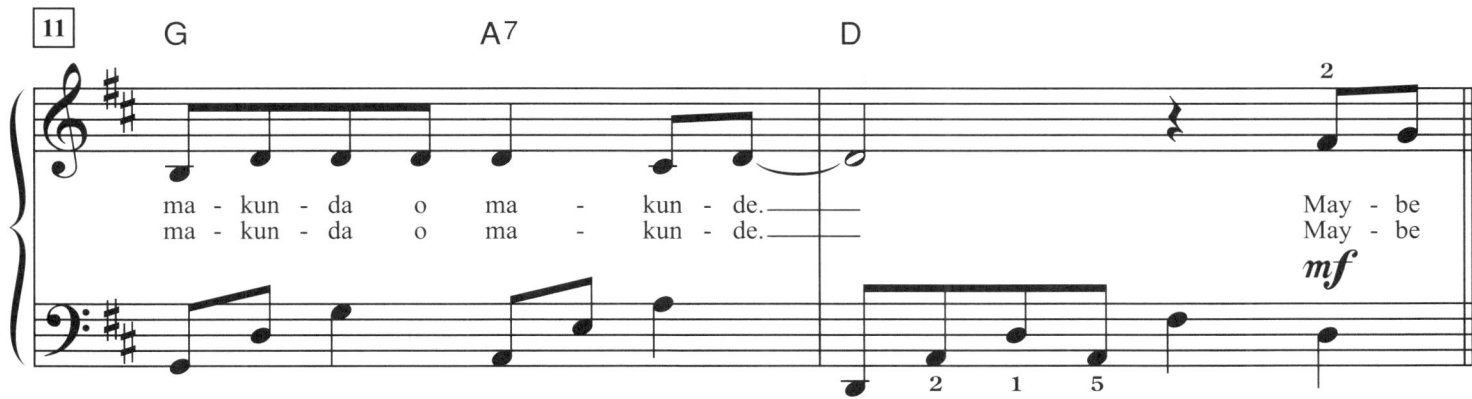
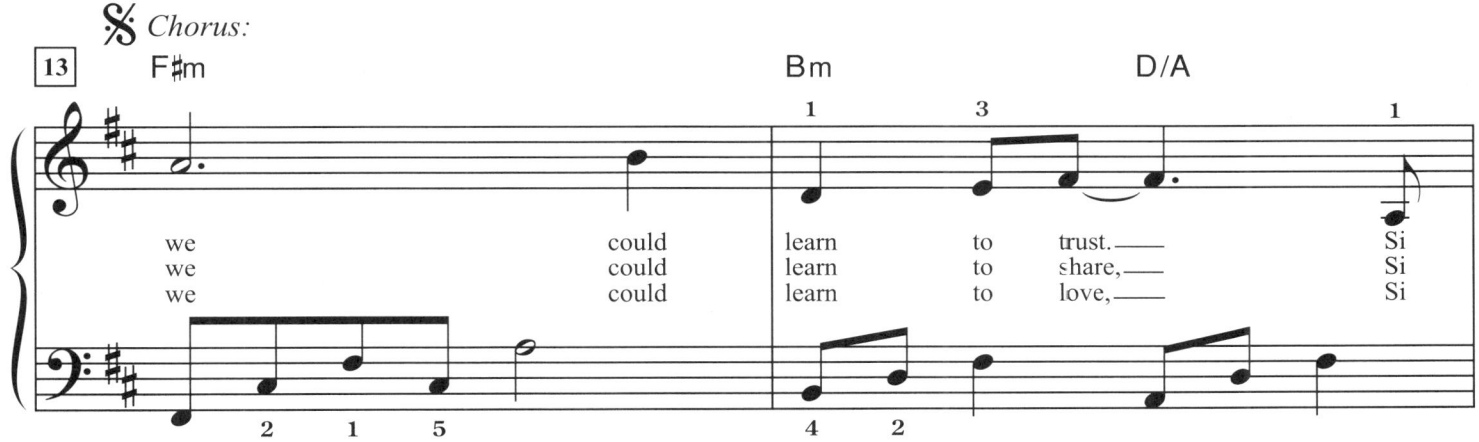
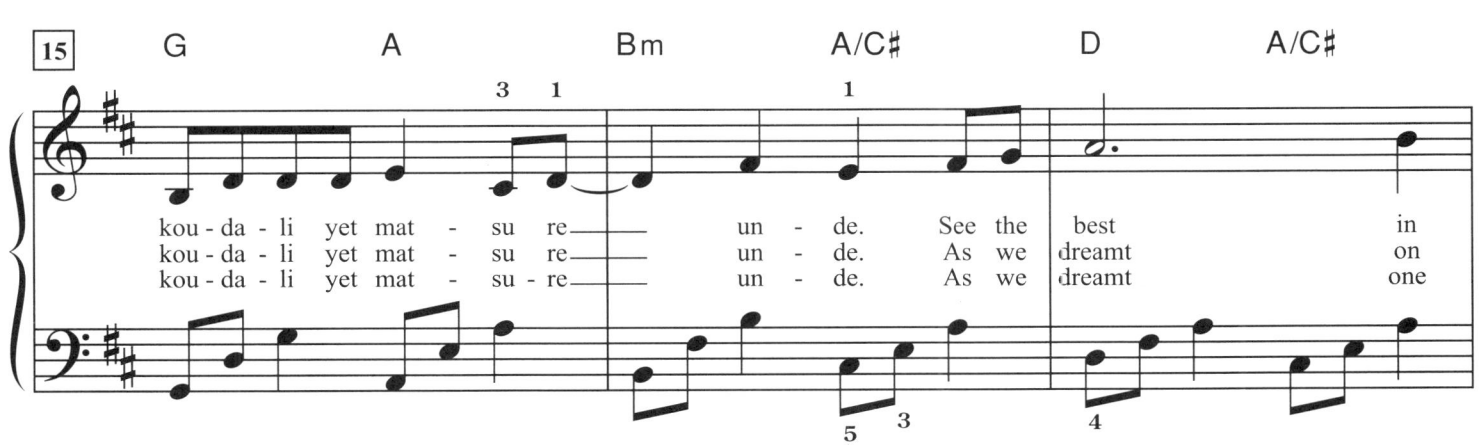

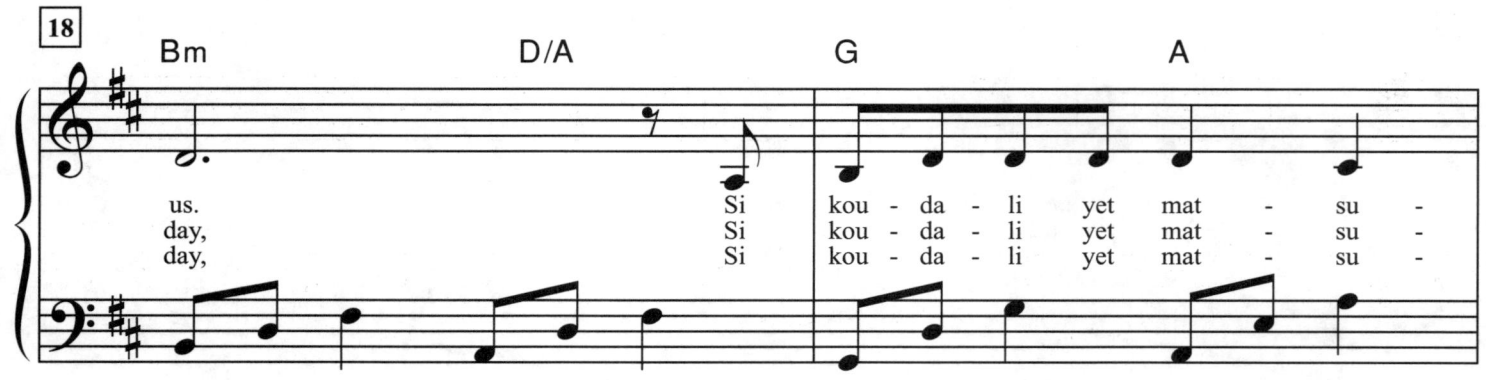
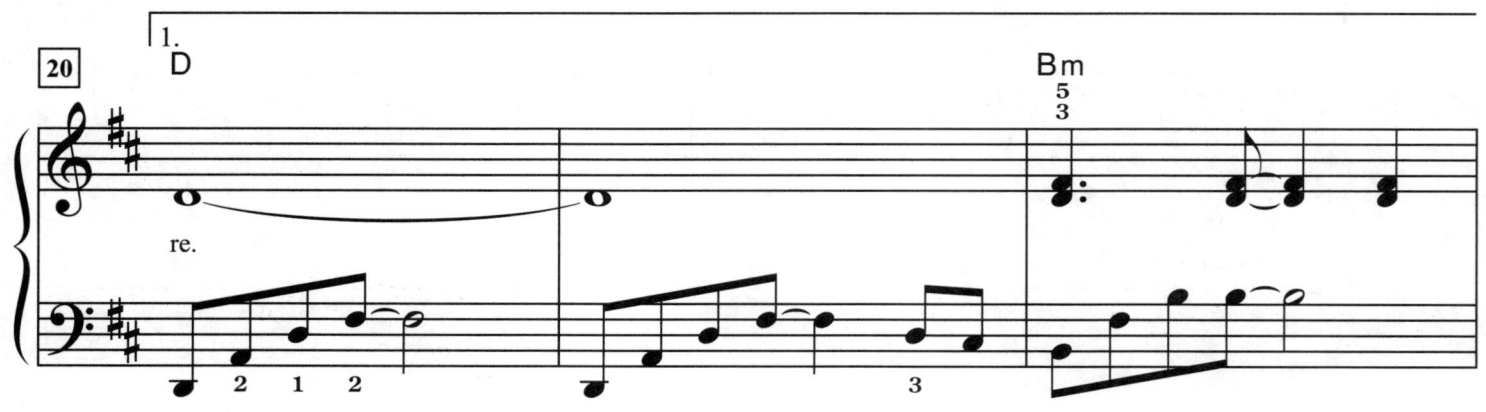
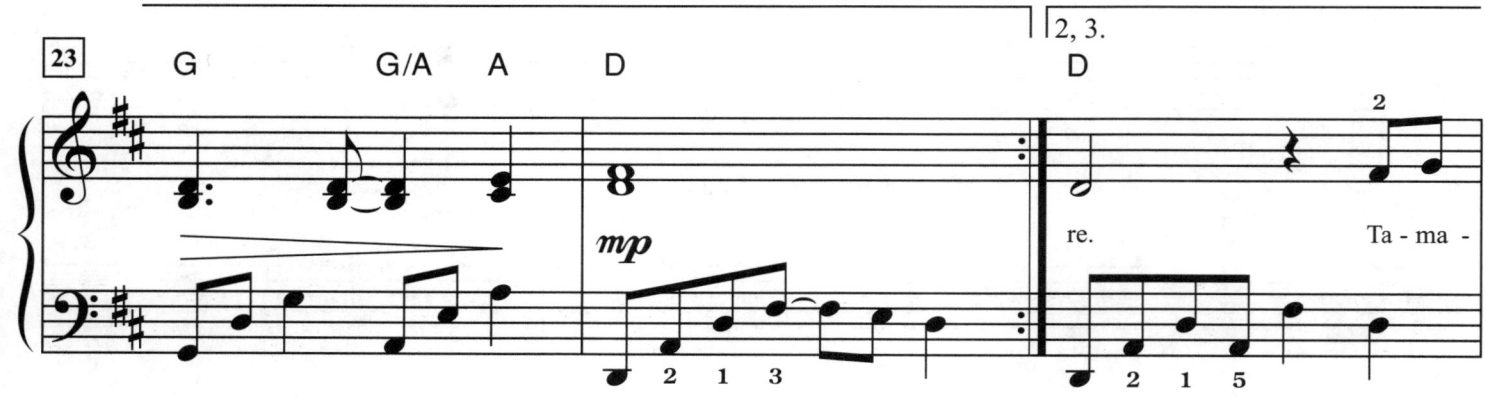
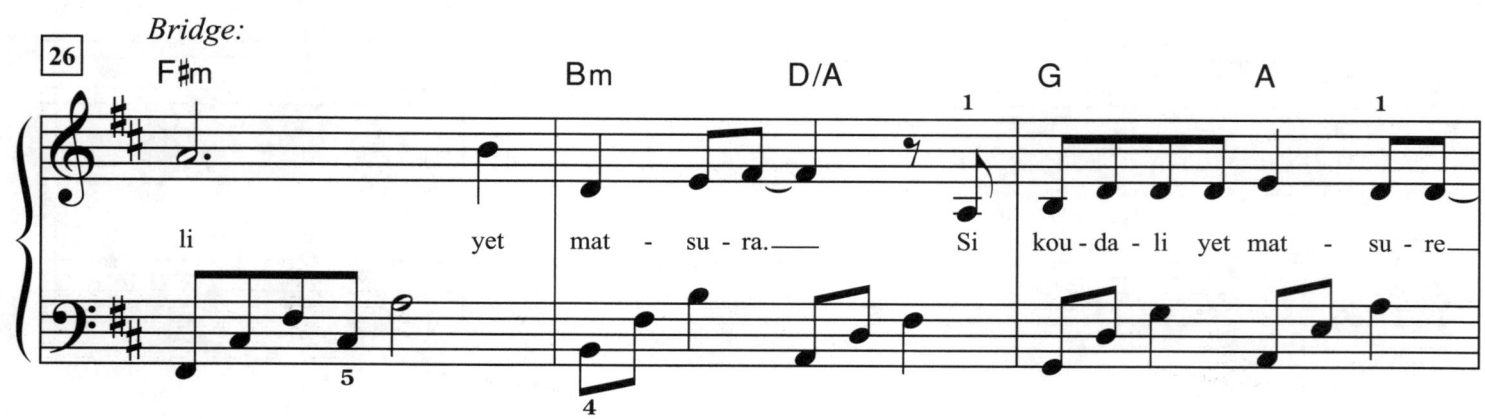

17

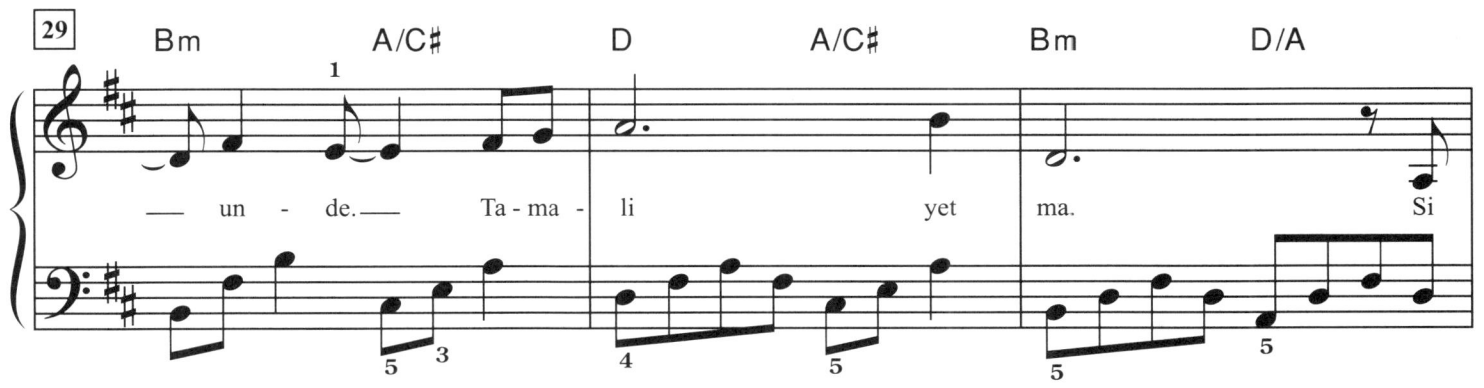

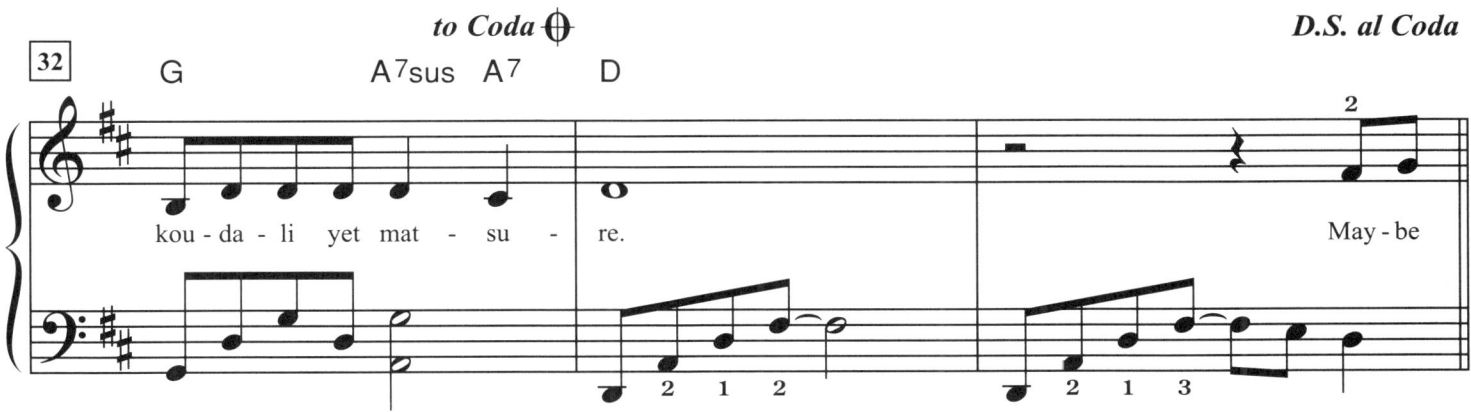

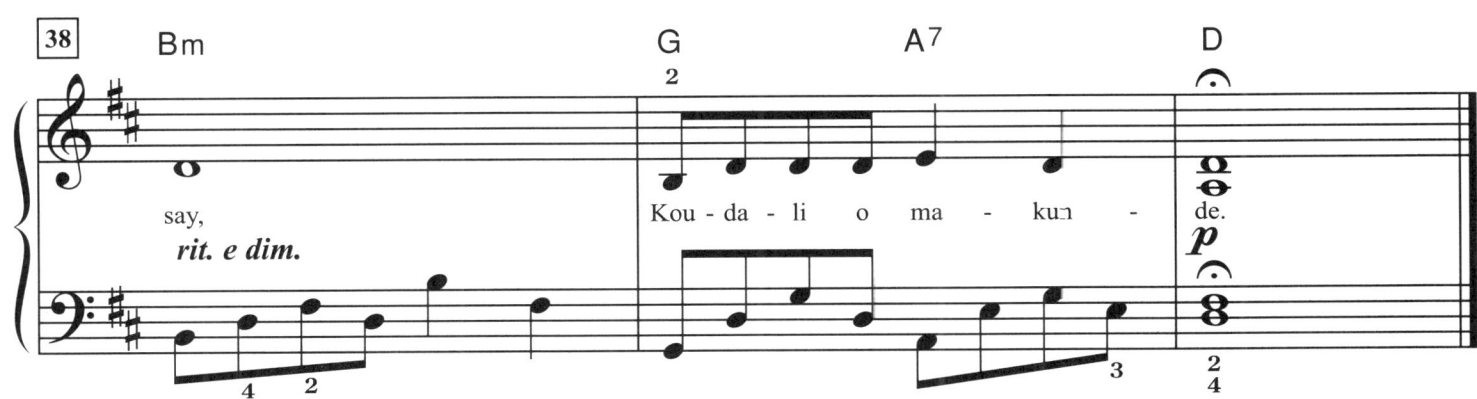

KUMBALAWÉ
(from "Saltimbanco")

Music by René Dupéré
Arranged by Dan Coates

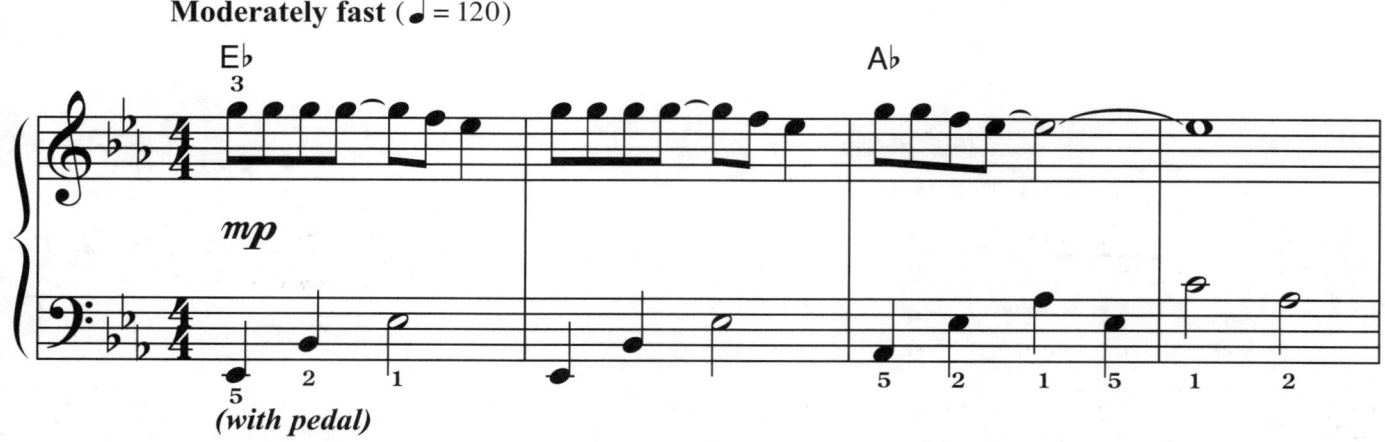

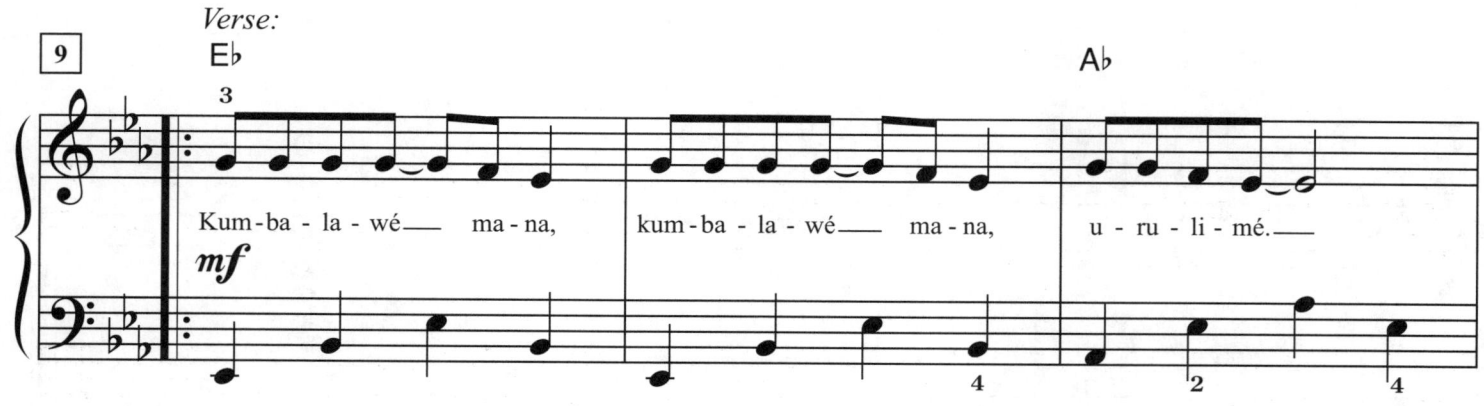

Kum - ba - la - wé — ma - na, kum - ba - la - wé — ma - na, u - ru - li - mé.—

© 1992 CRÉATIONS MÉANDRES INC.
All Rights Reserved

19

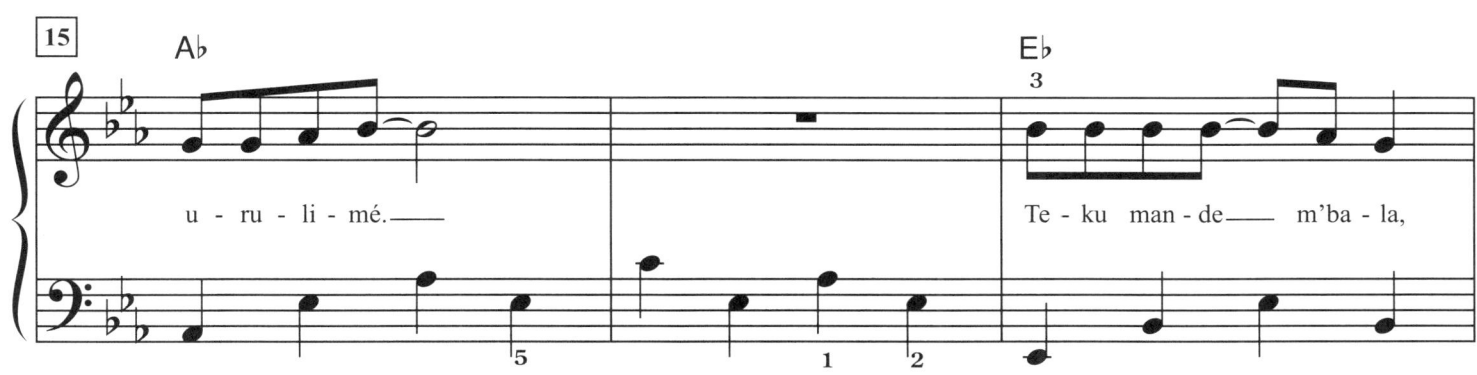
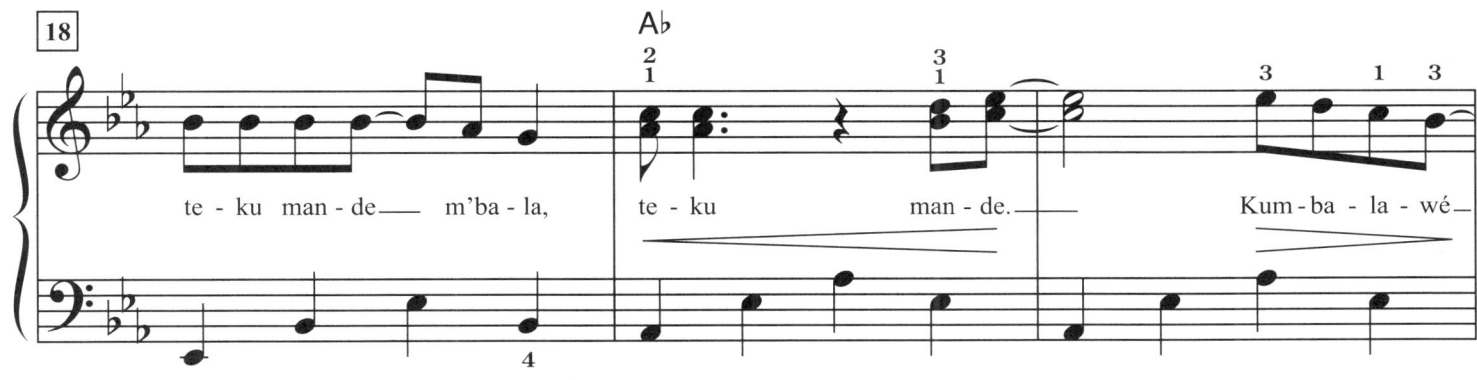
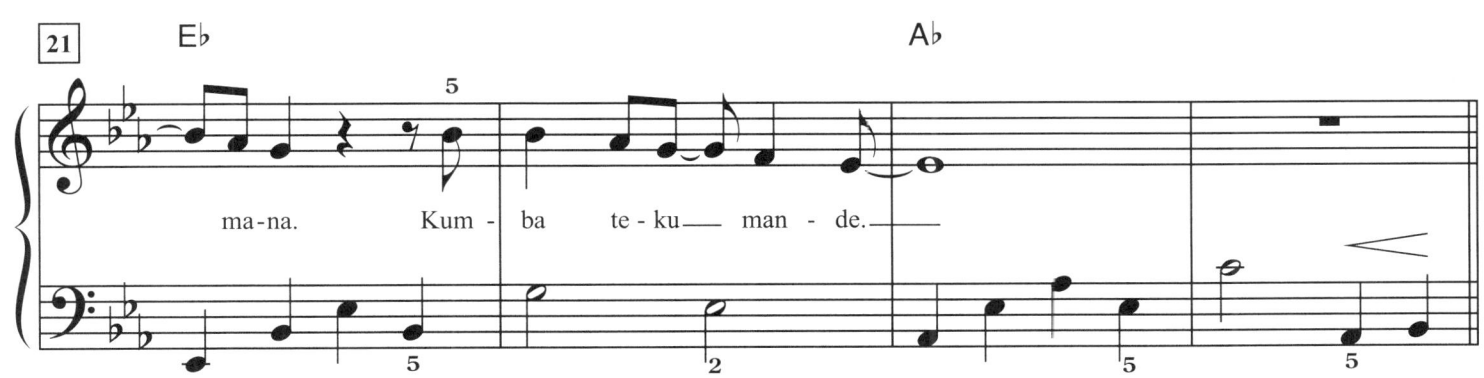

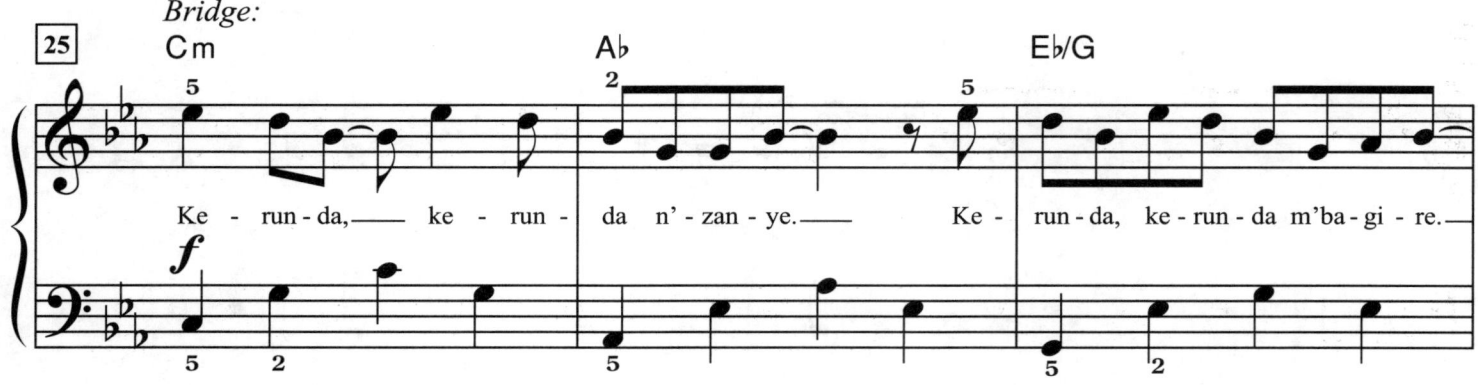
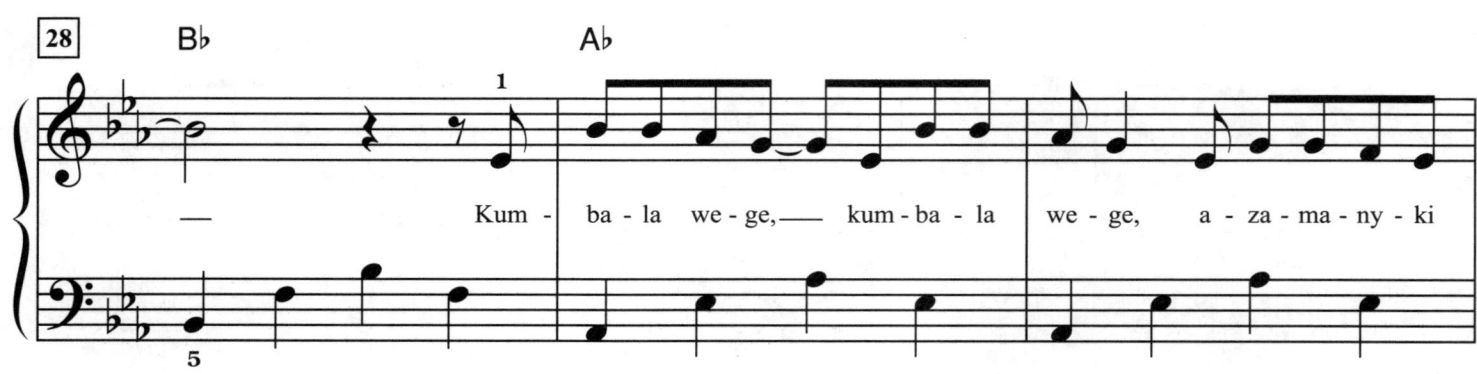
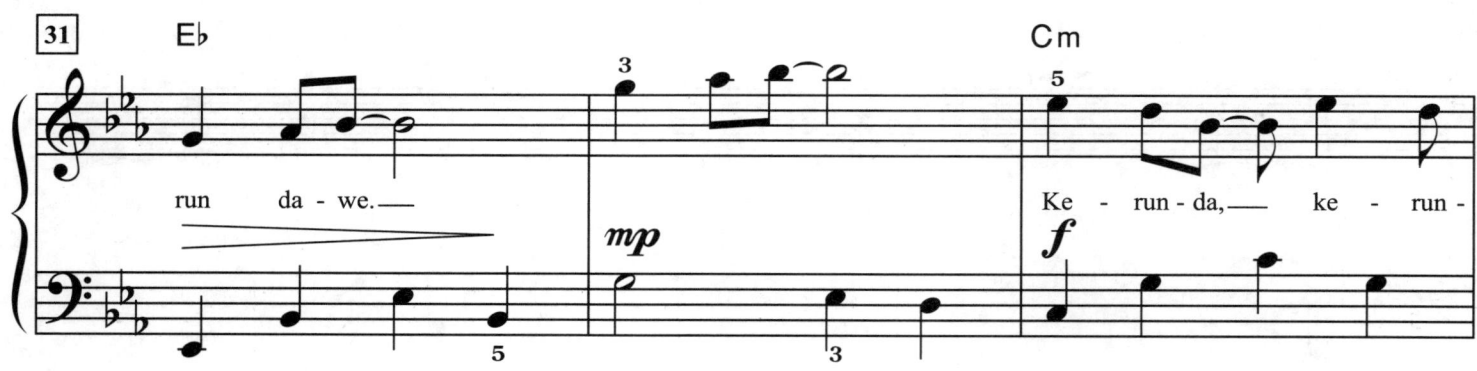

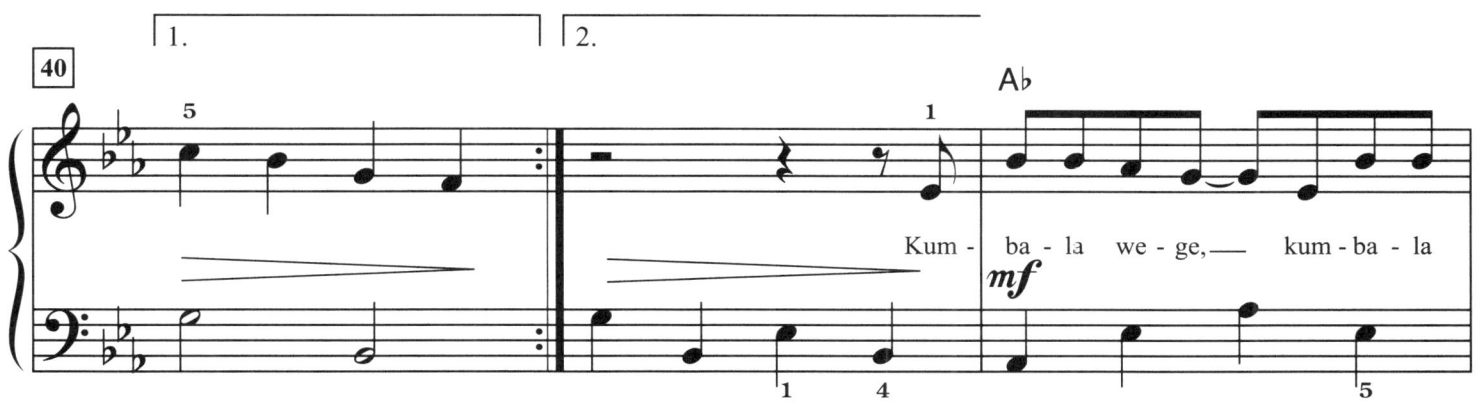
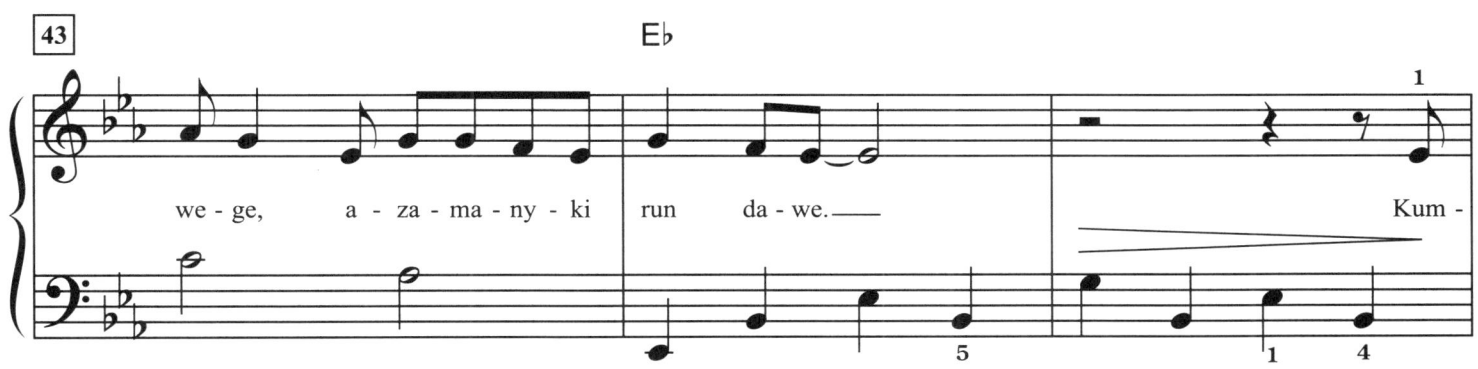

KUNYA SOBÉ
(from "Mystère Live")

Composed by René Dupéré
Arranged by Dan Coates

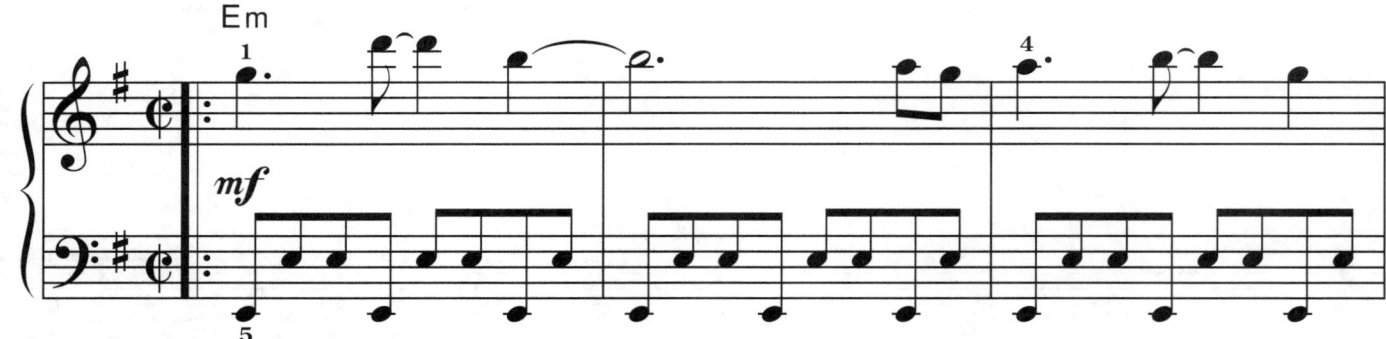

© 1996 CRÉATIONS MÉANDRES INC.
All Rights Reserved

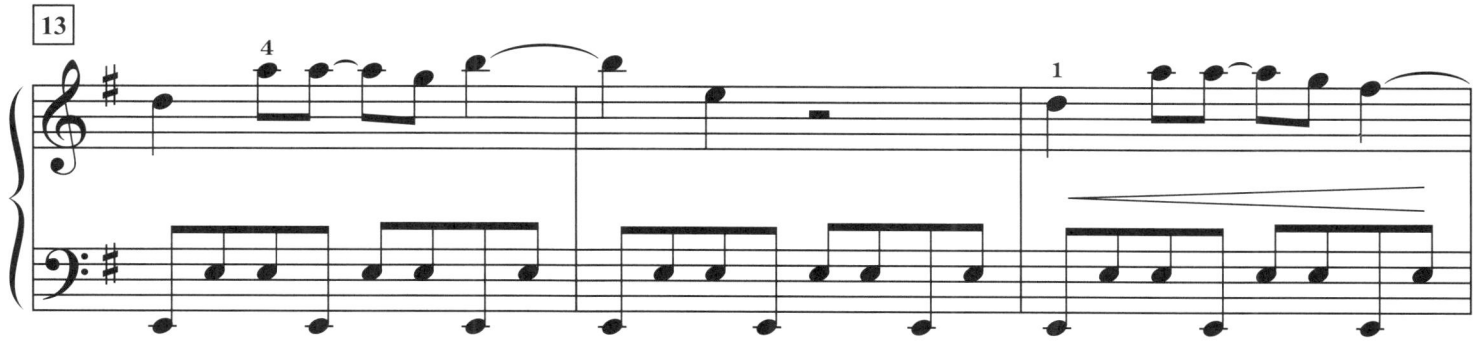

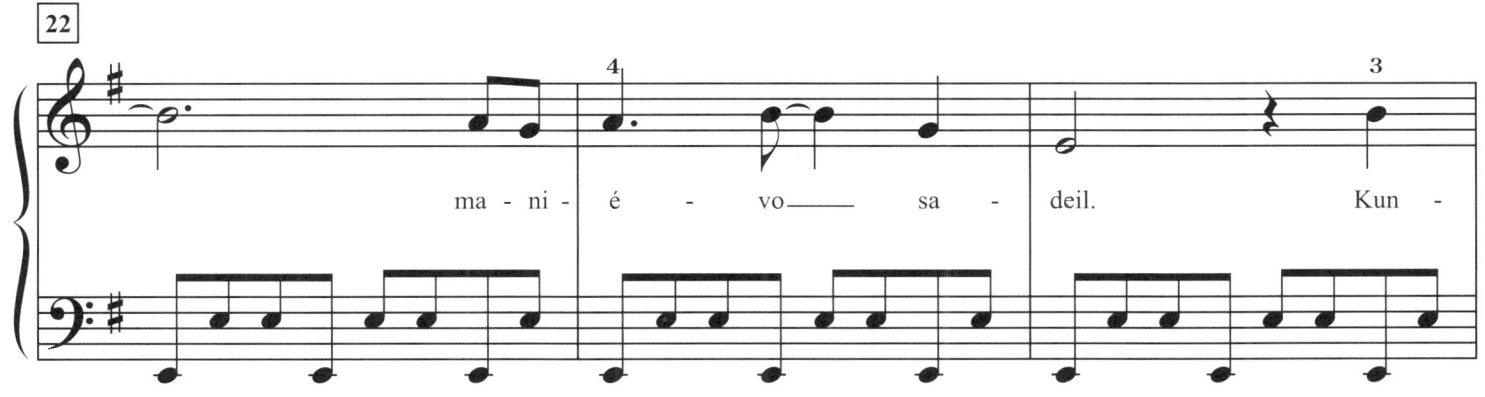

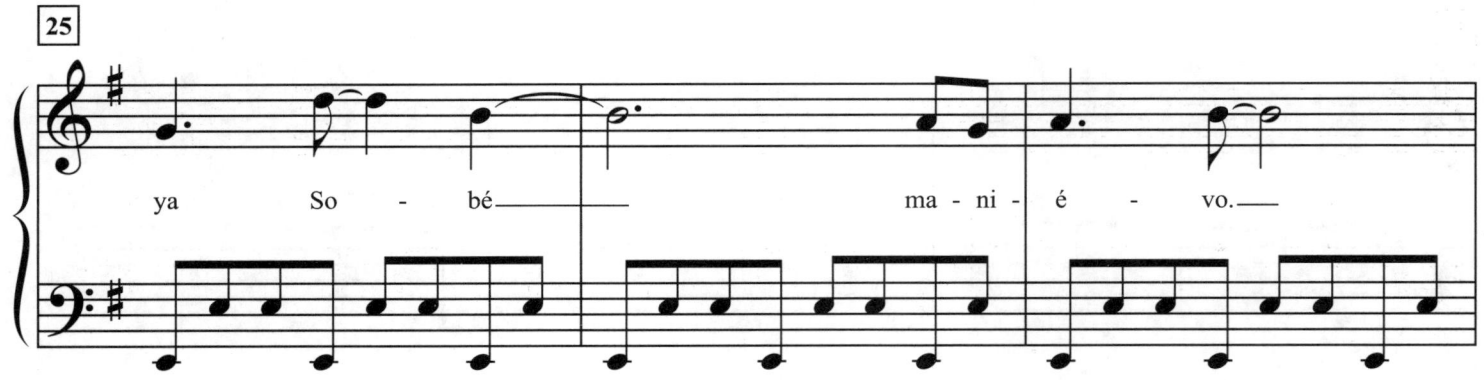
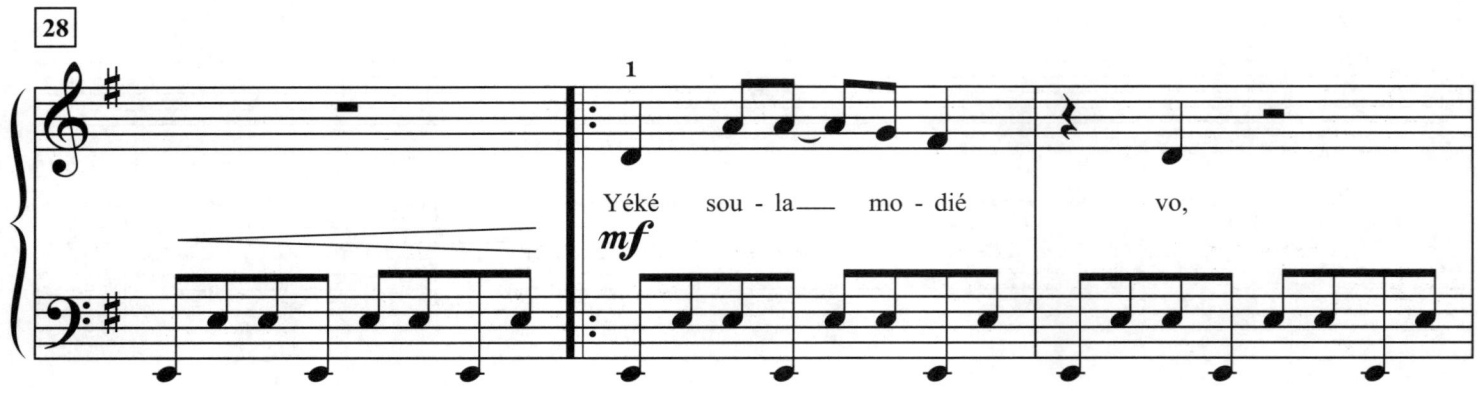

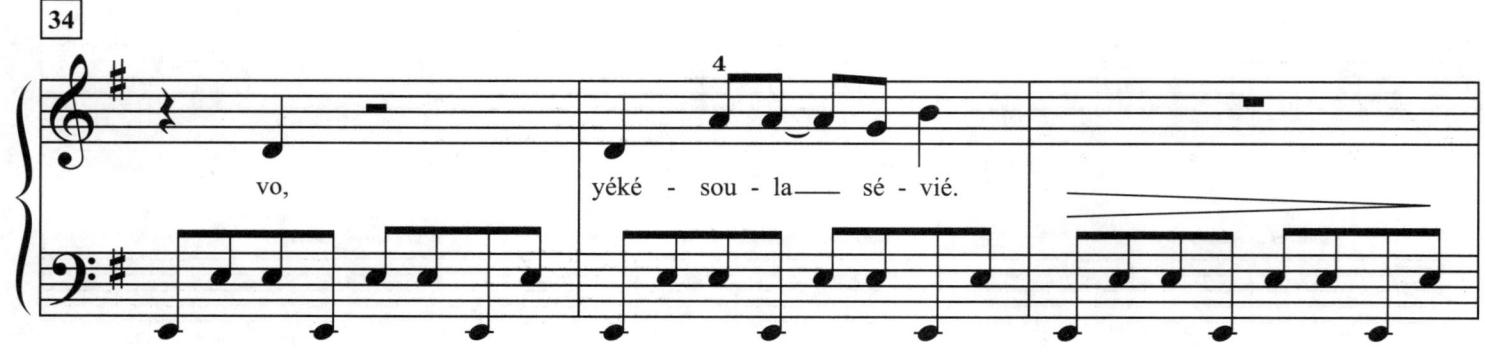

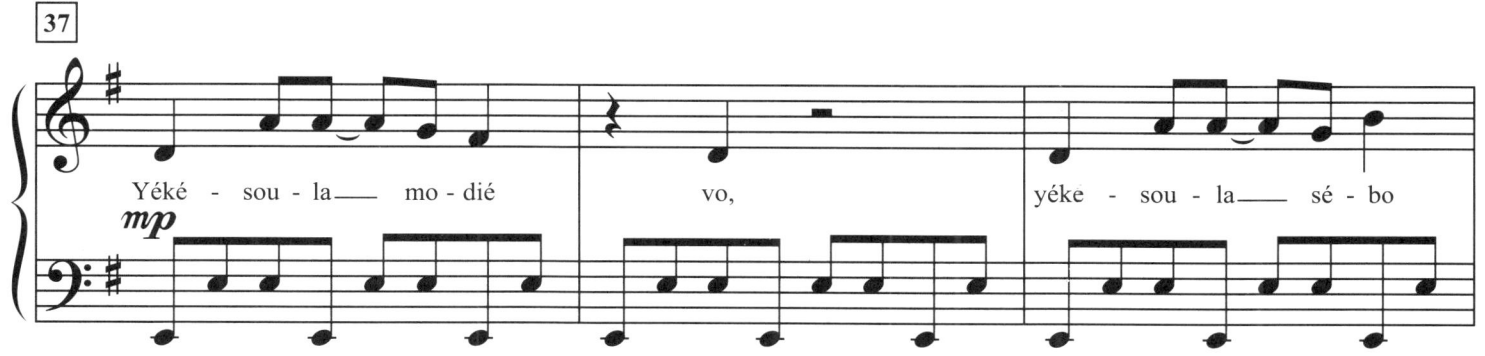

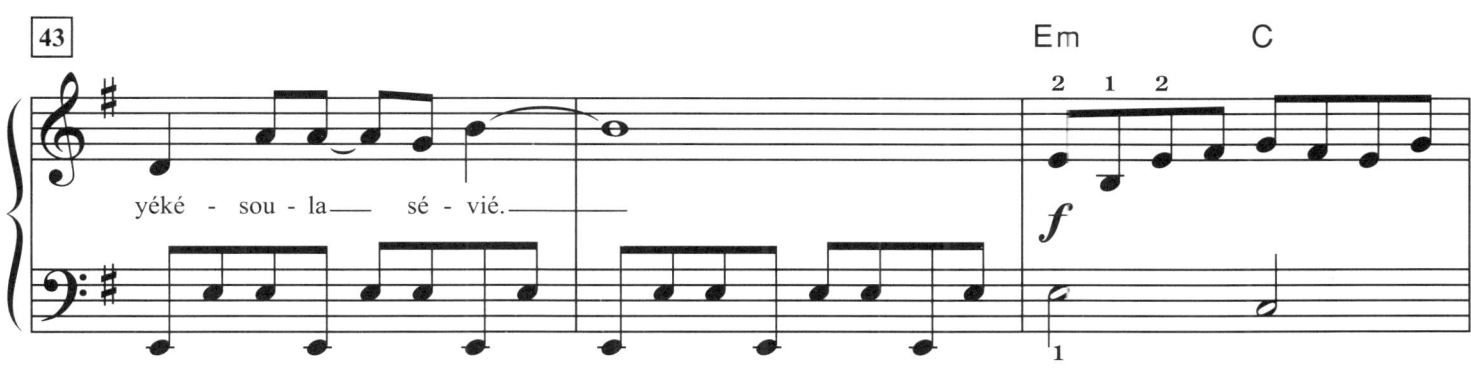
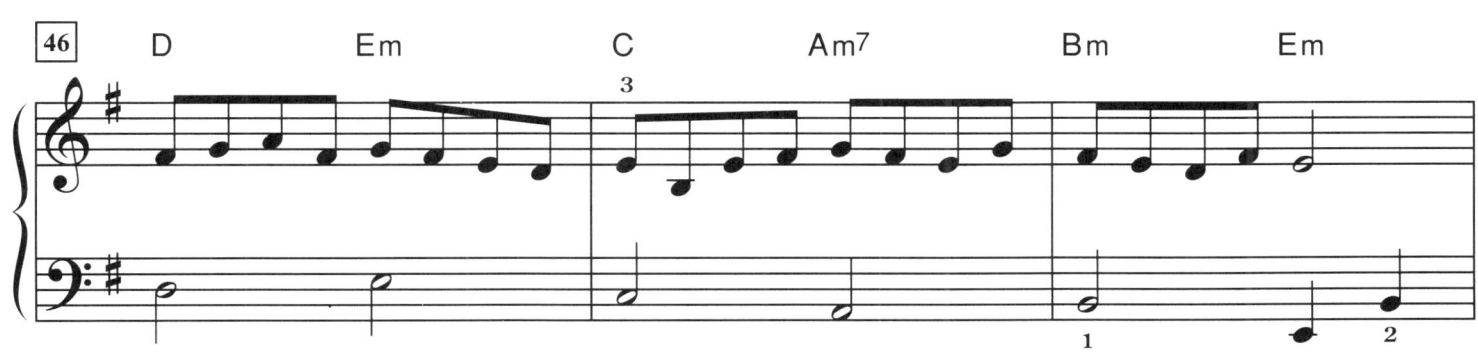

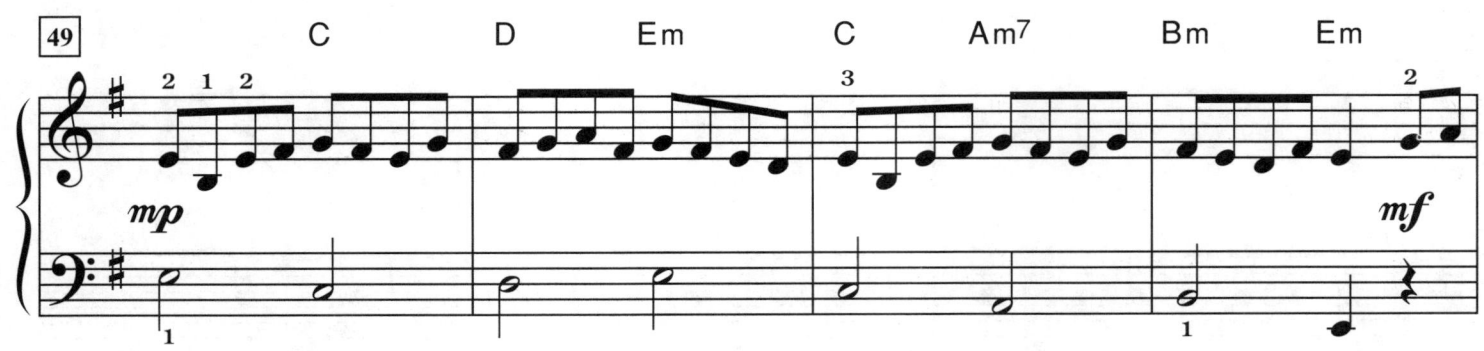

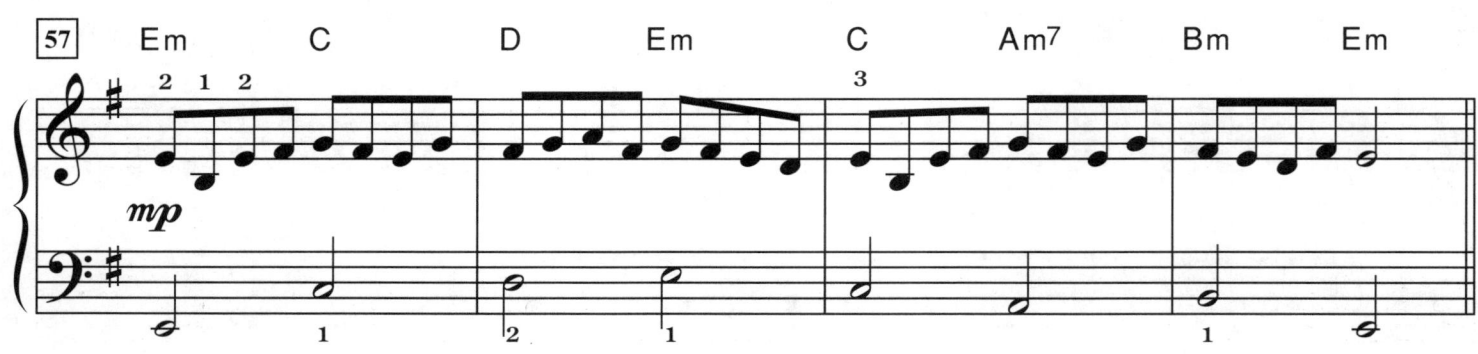
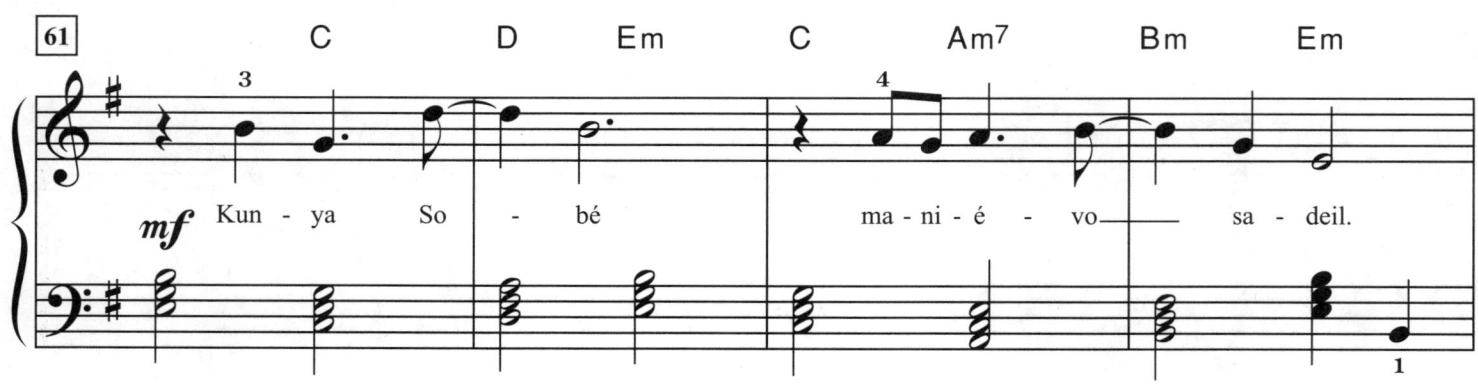

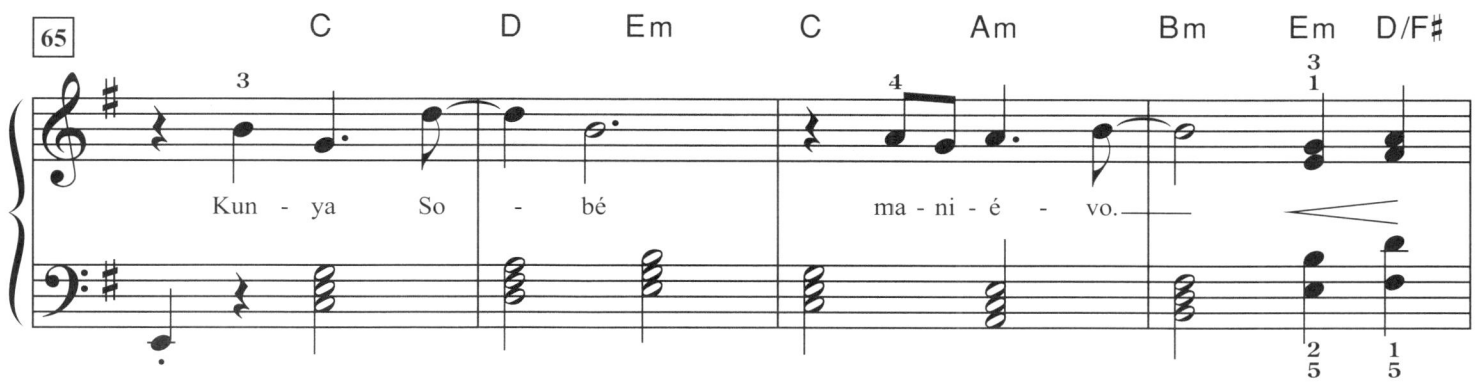
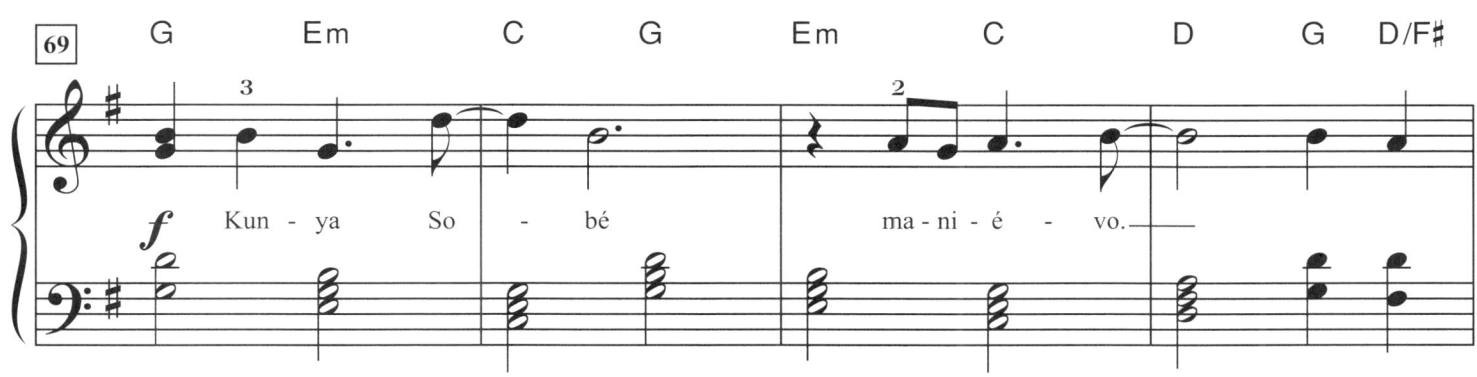
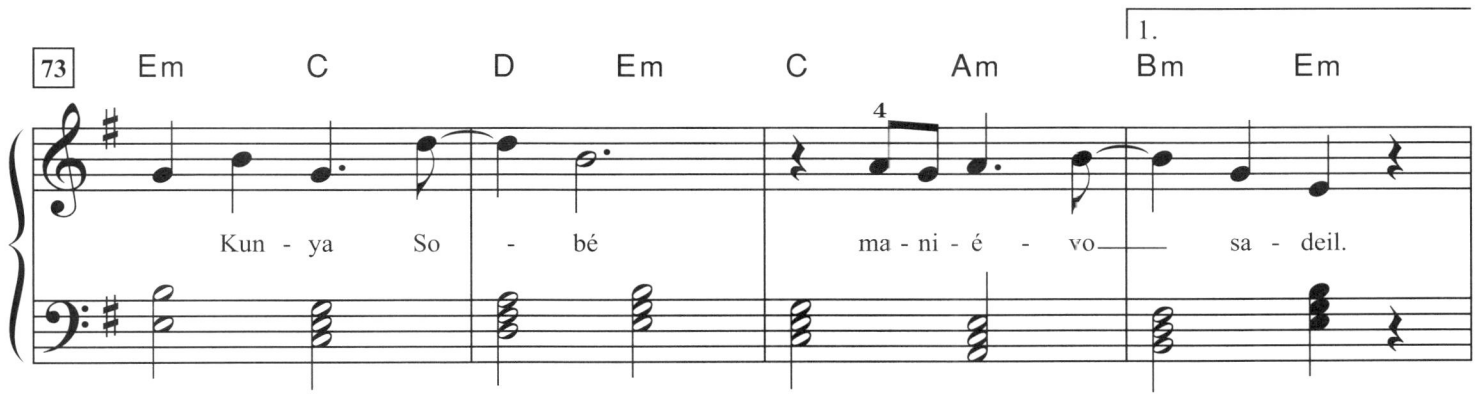

LOVE DANCE
(from "KÀ")

Music by René Dupéré
Arranged by Dan Coates

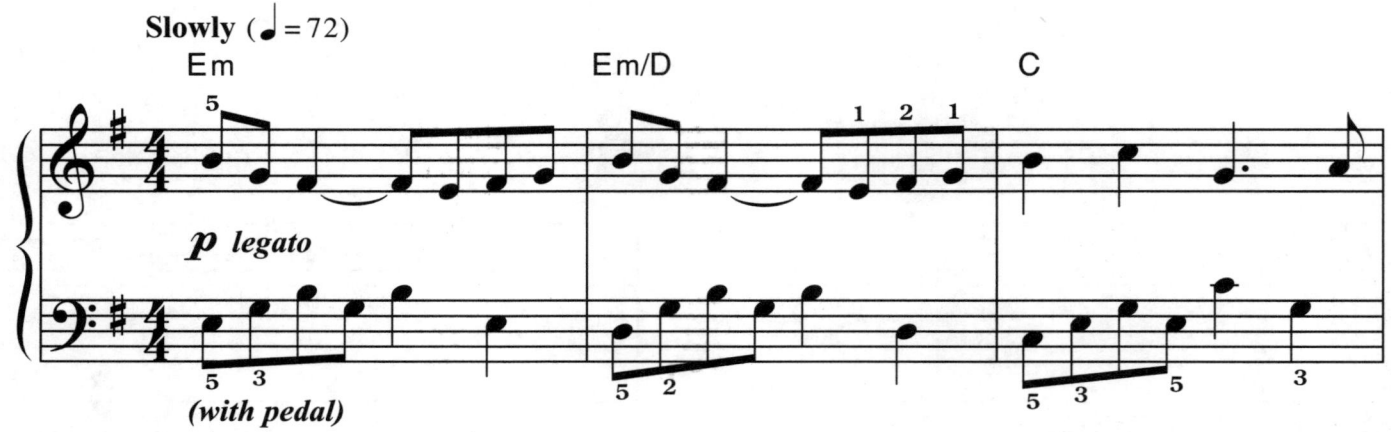

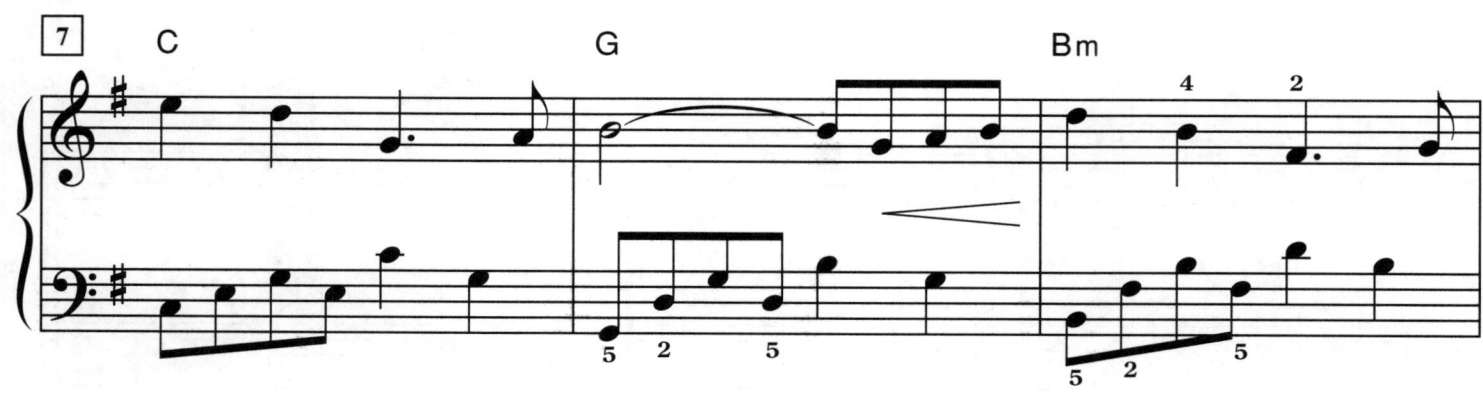

© 2005 CRÉATIONS MÉANDRES INC.
All Rights Reserved

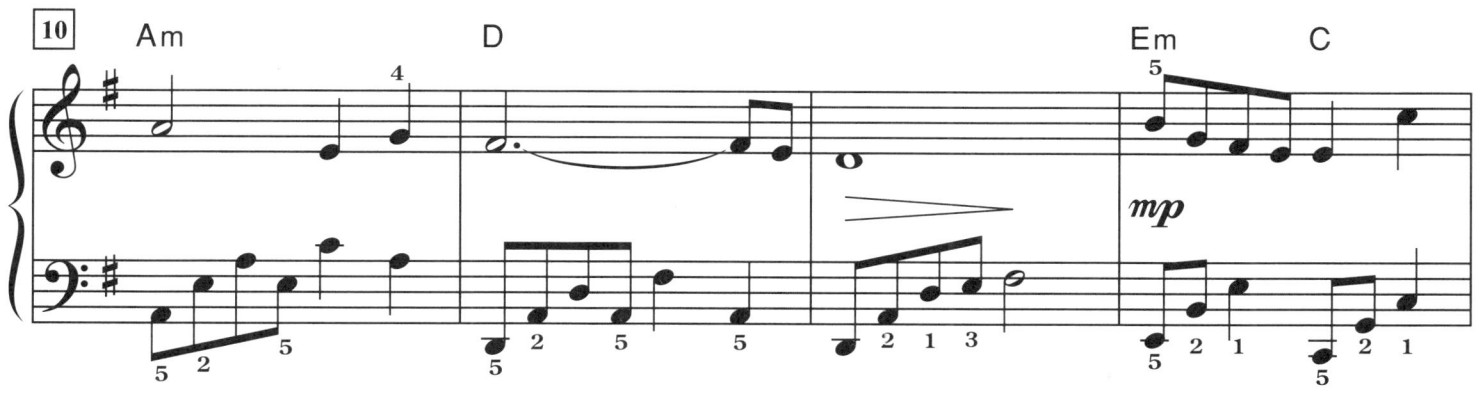
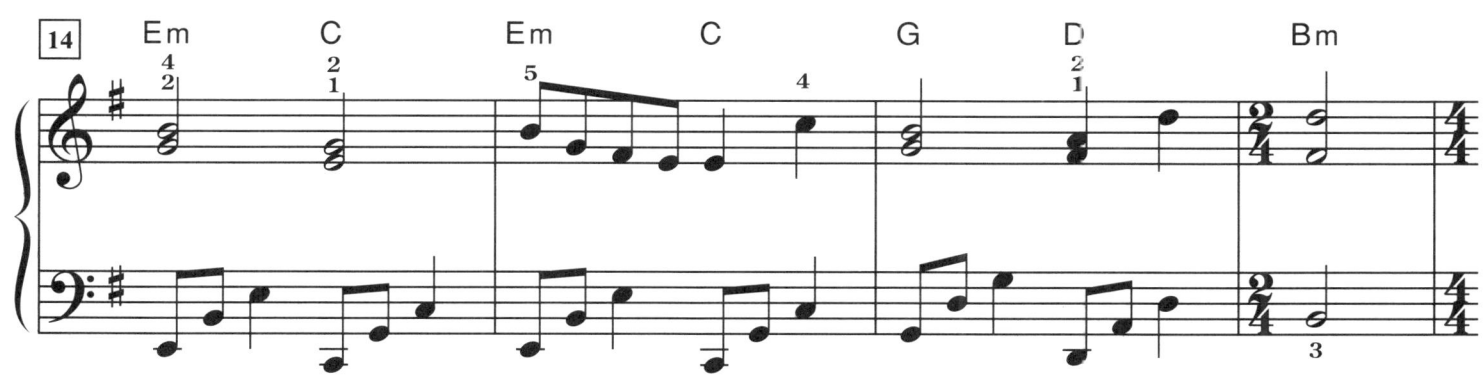
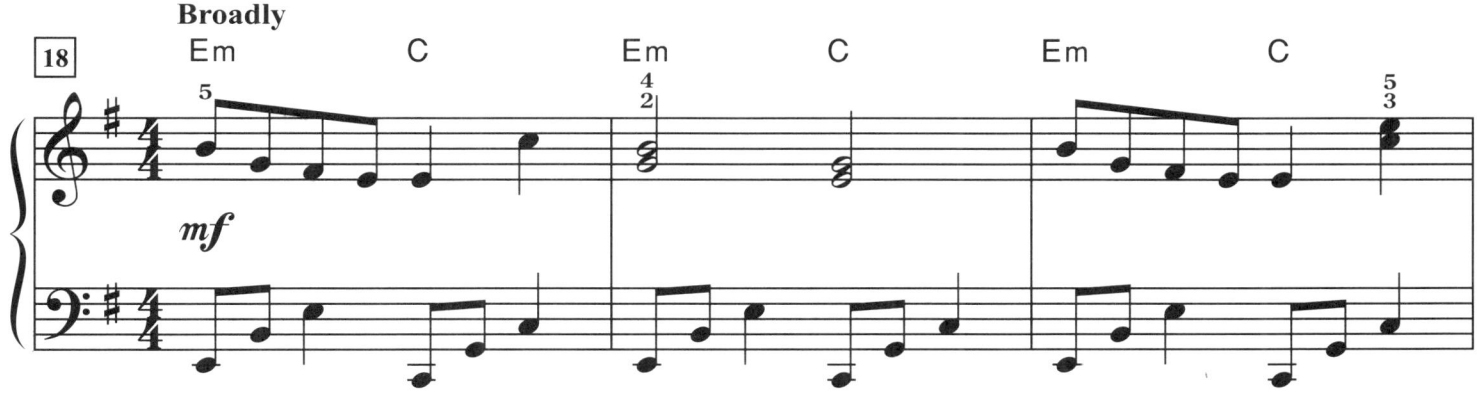

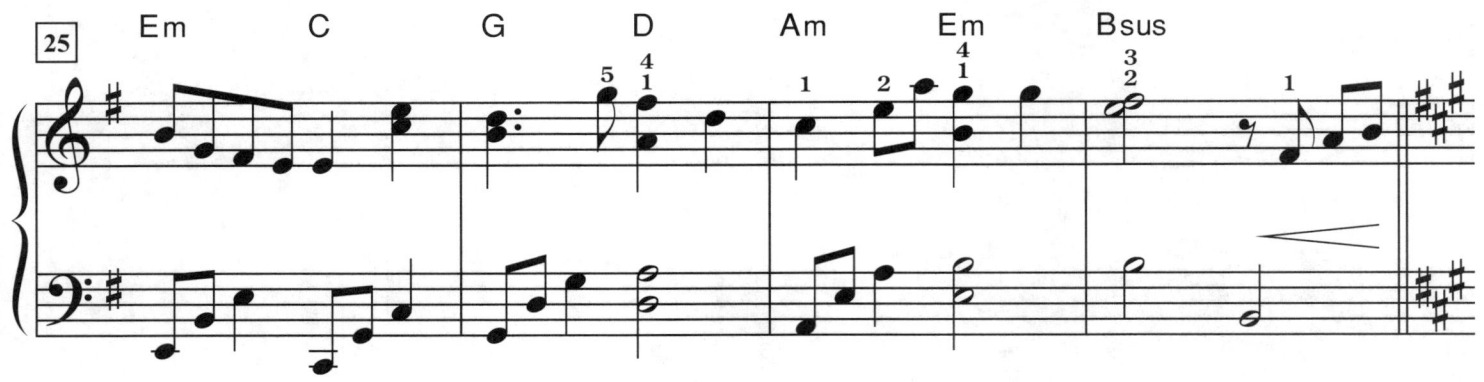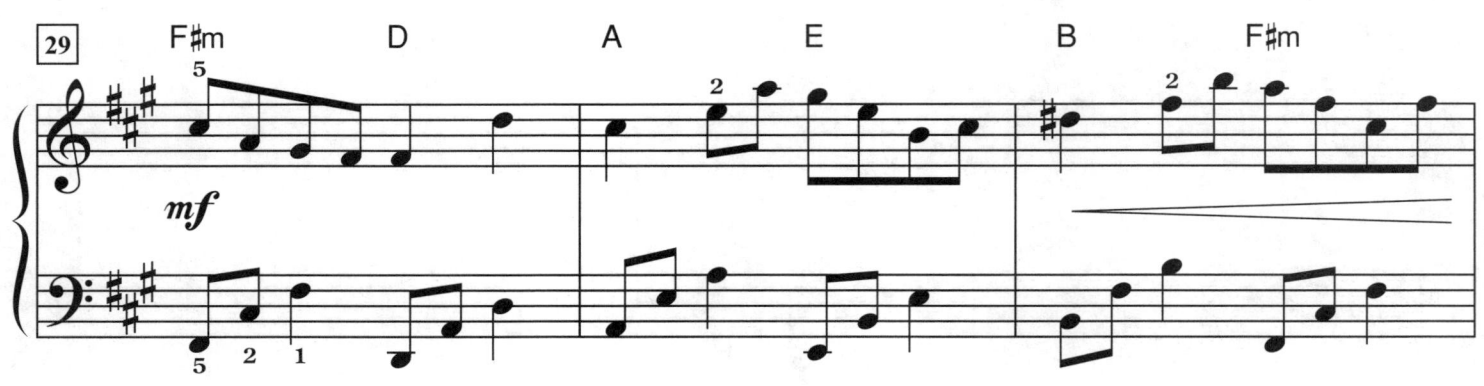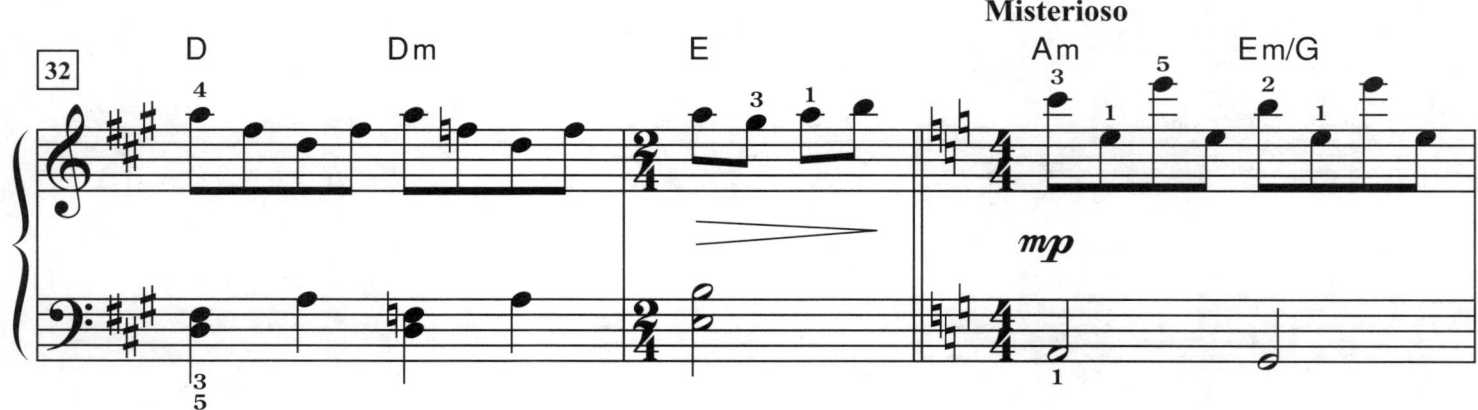

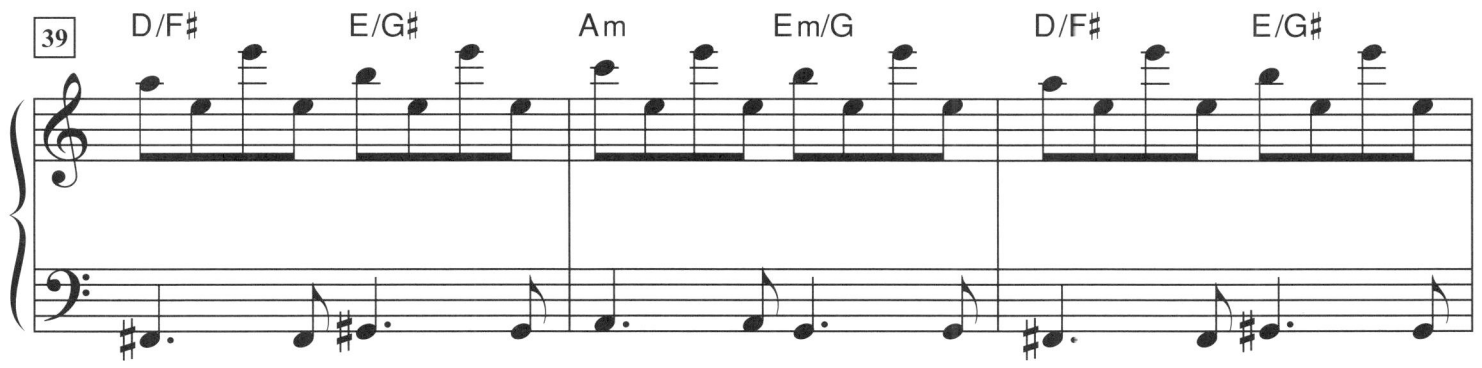
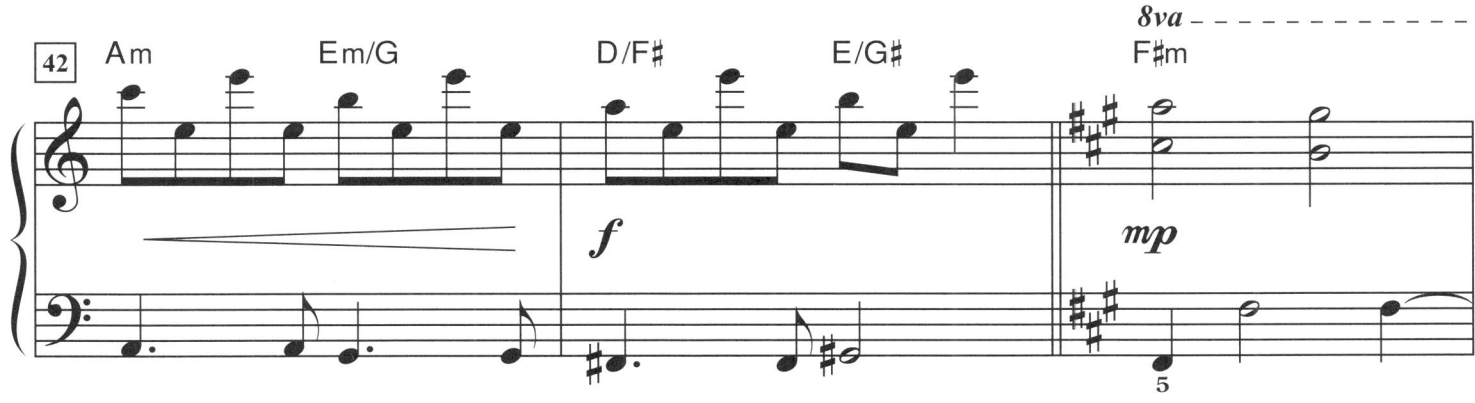
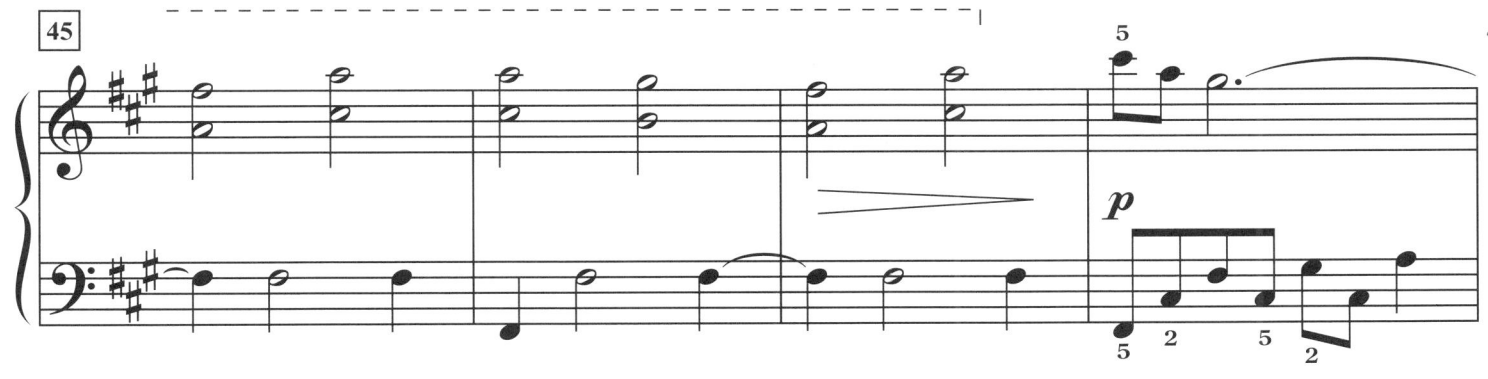
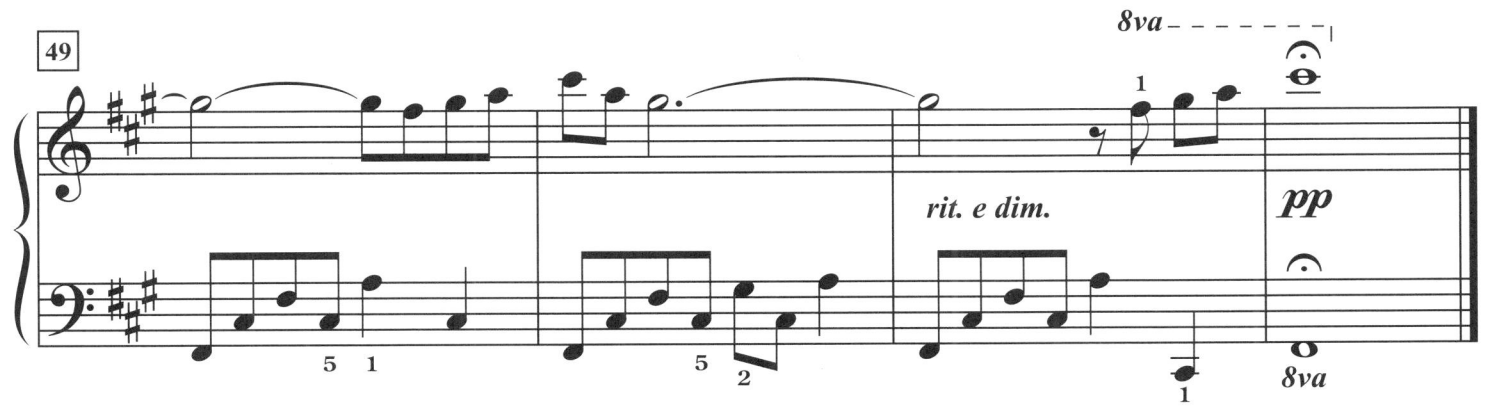

MIO BELLO BELLO AMORE
(from "Zumanity: Another Side of Cirque du Soleil")

Composed by Simon Carpentier
Lyrics by Anna Liani
Arranged by Dan Coates

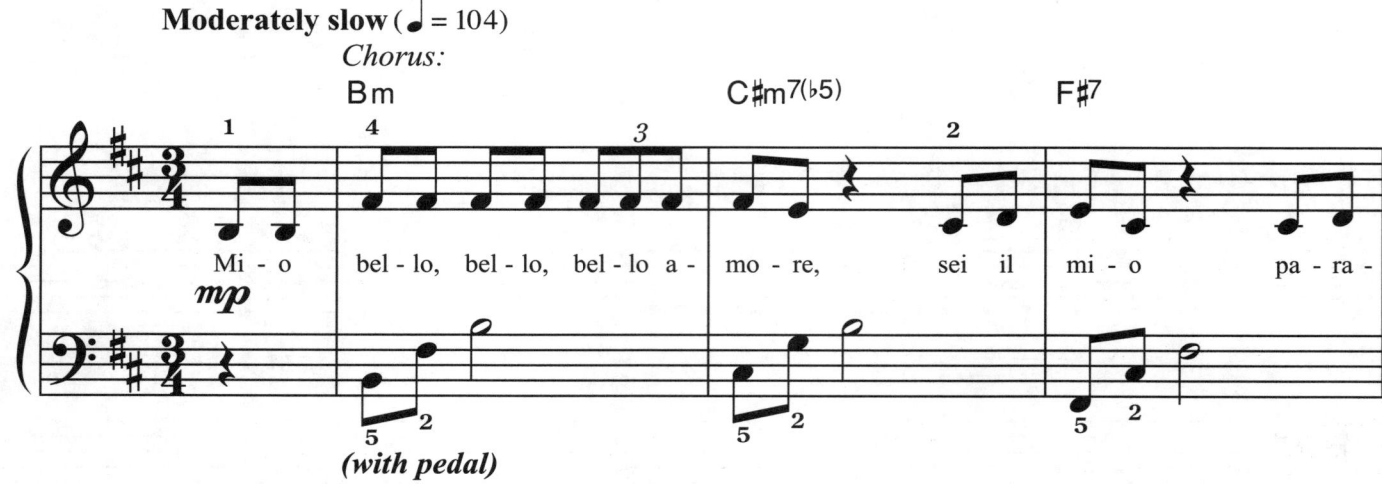
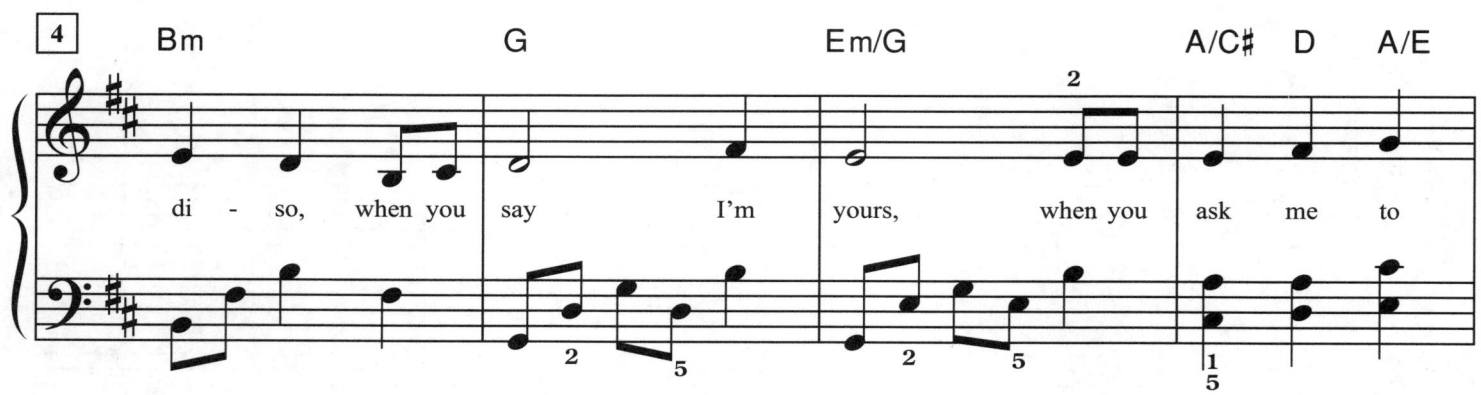
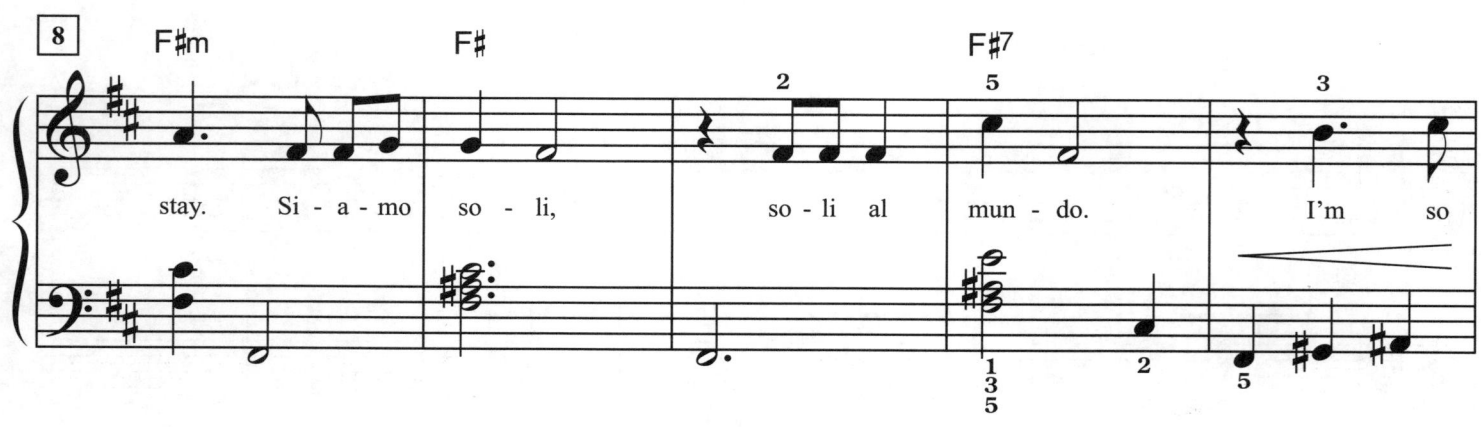

© 2004 CRÉATIONS MÉANDRES INC.
All Rights Reserved

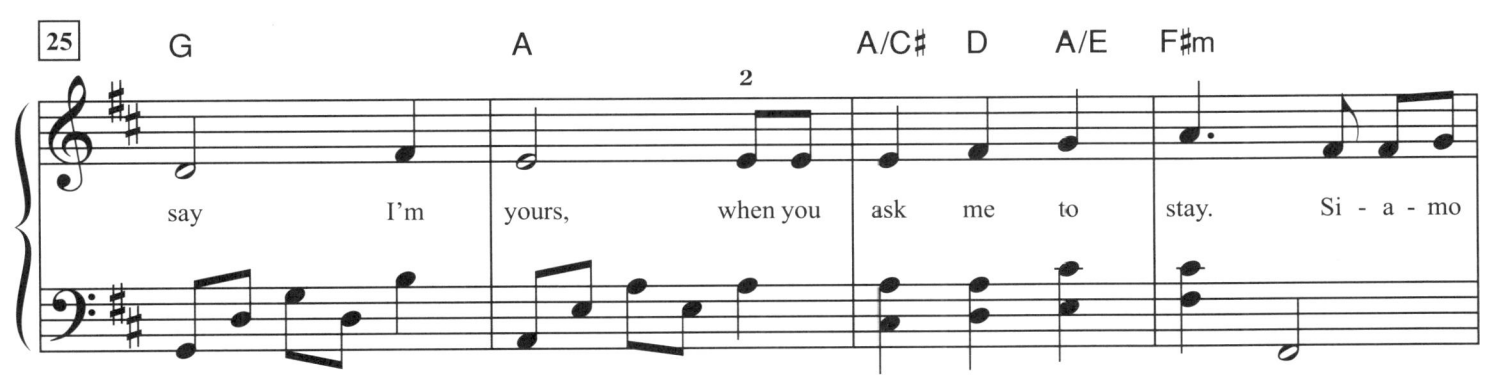

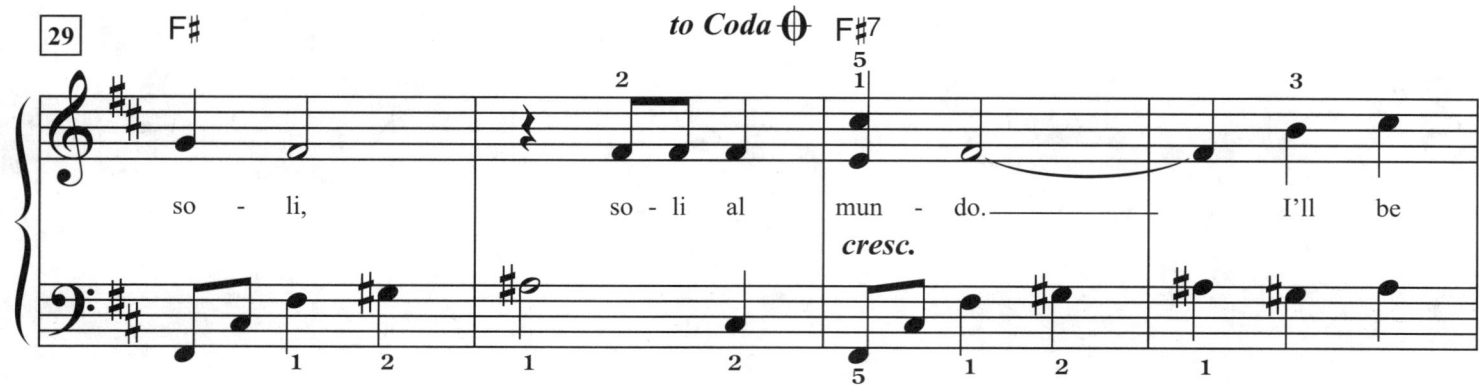
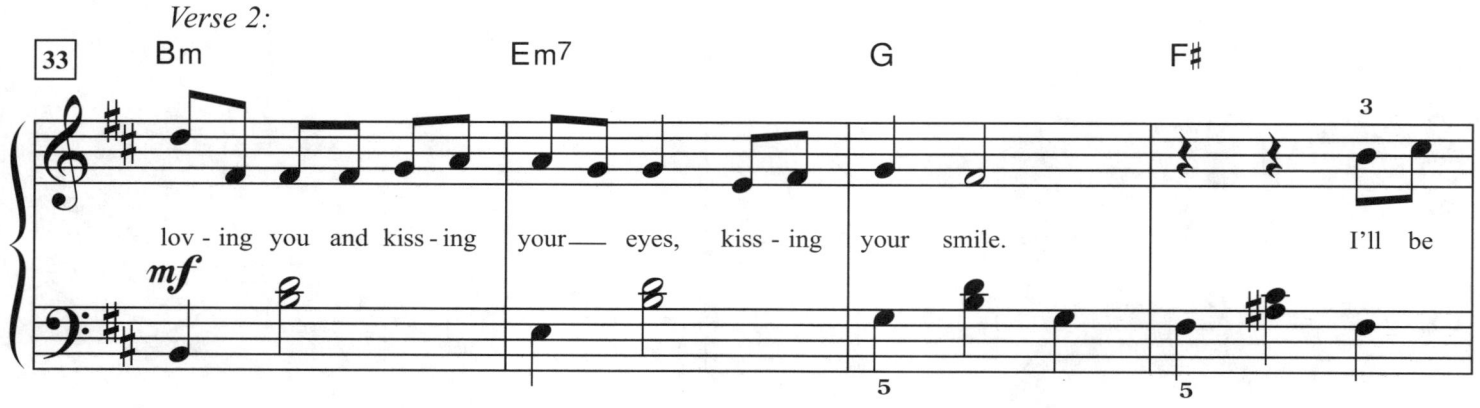

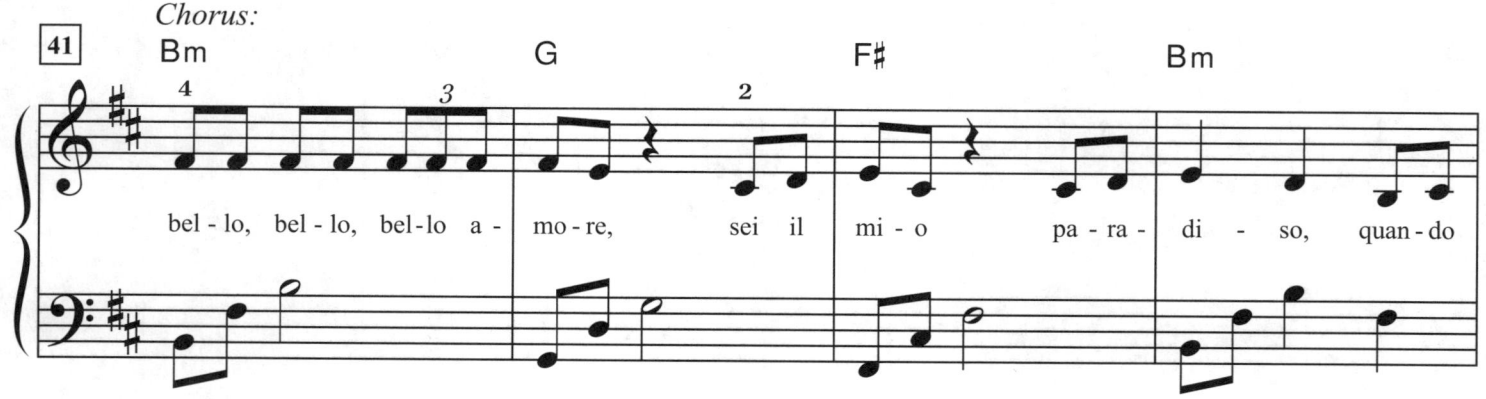

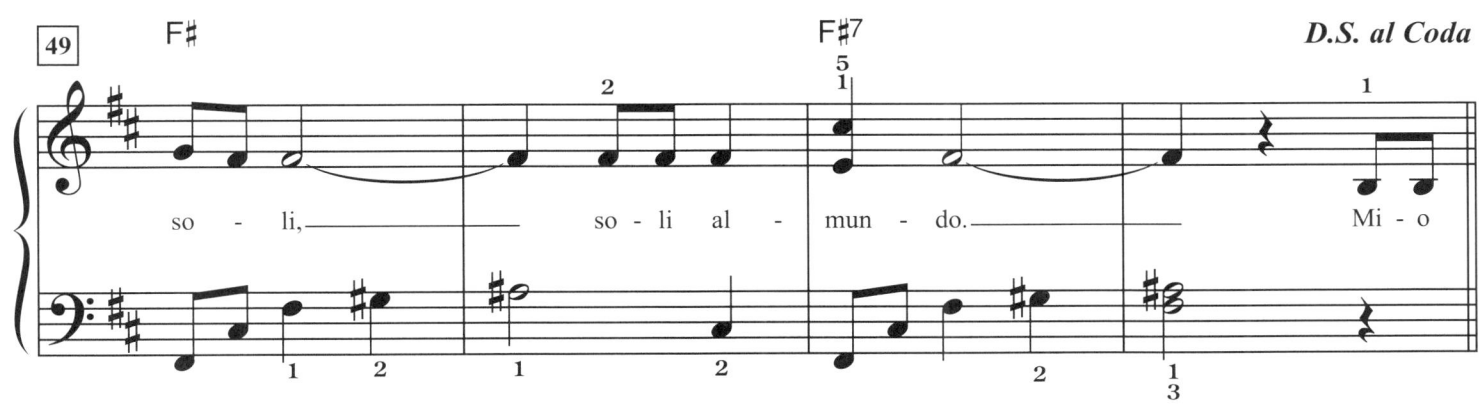

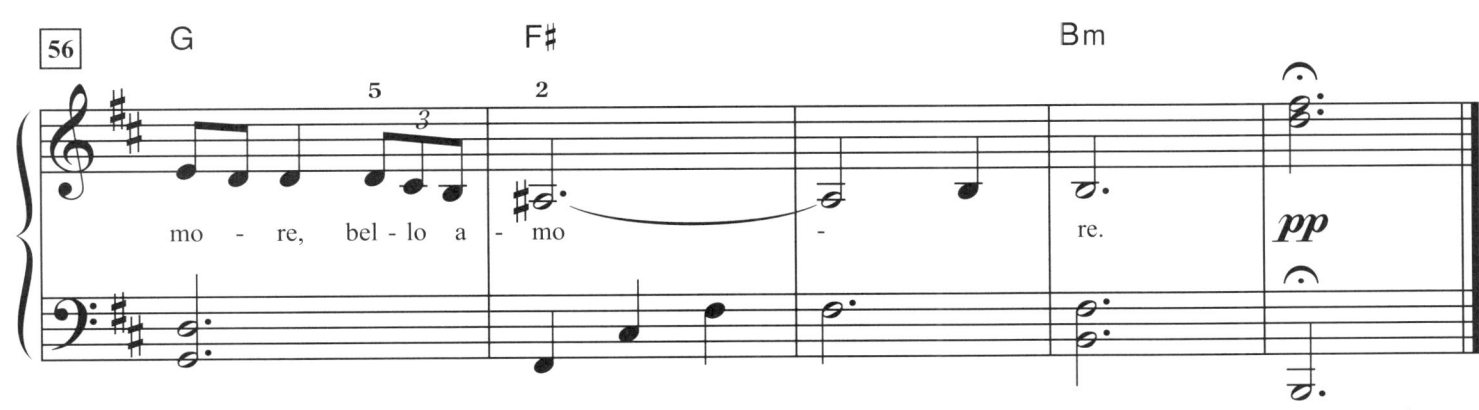

NOSTALGIE
(from "O")

Composed by Benoit Jutras
Arranged by Dan Coates

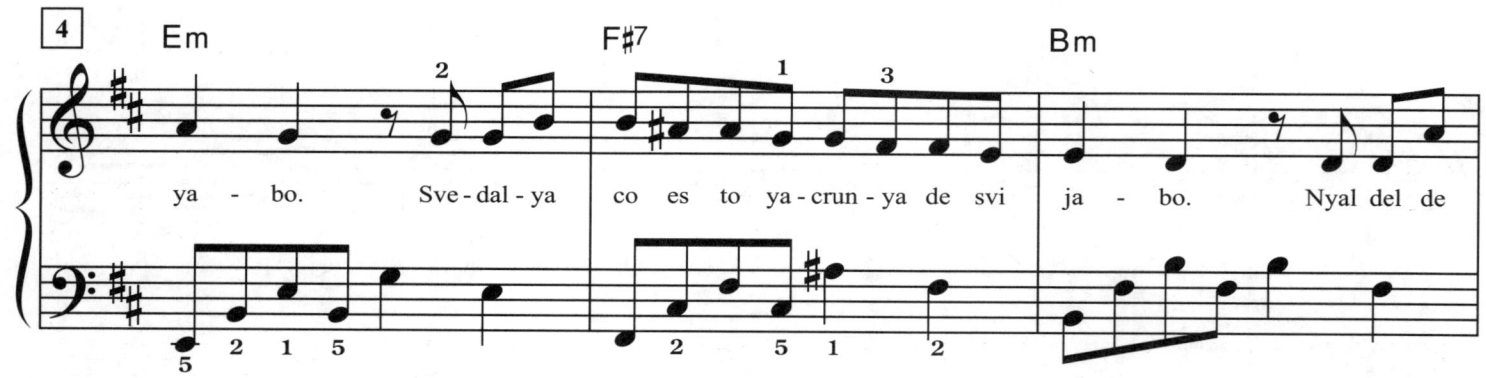

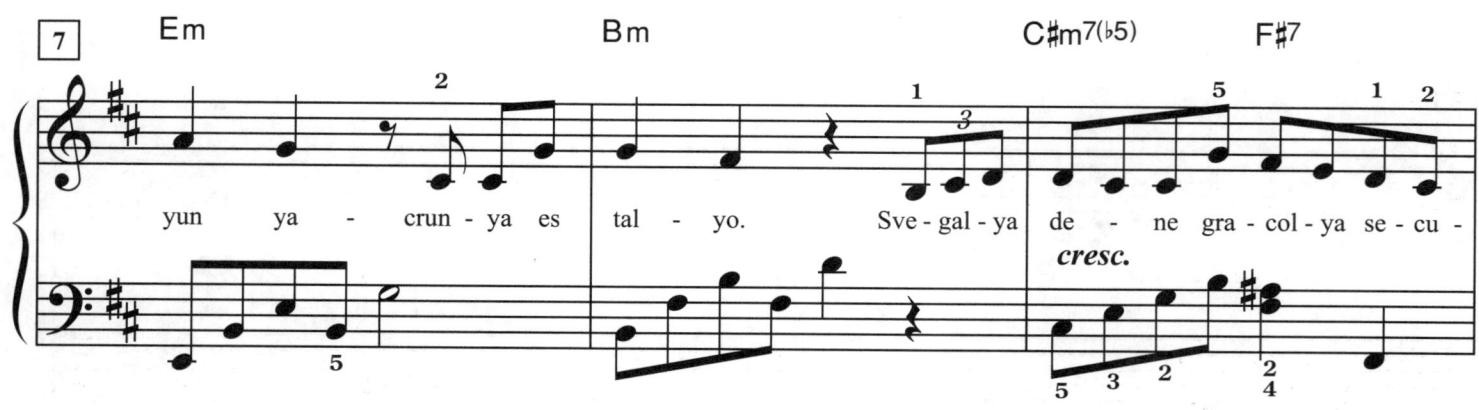

© 1998 CRÉATIONS MÉANDRES INC.
All Rights Reserved

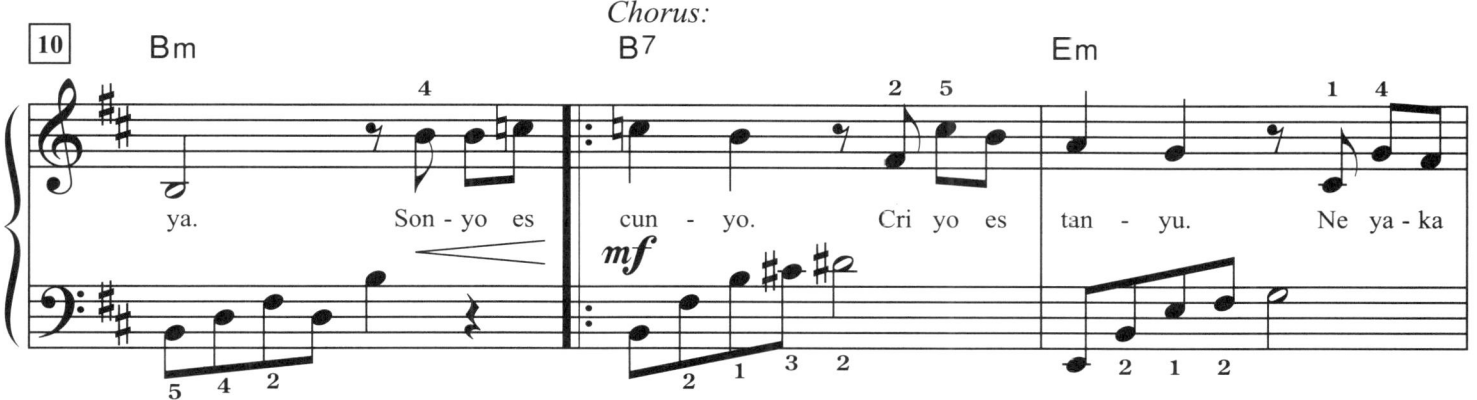
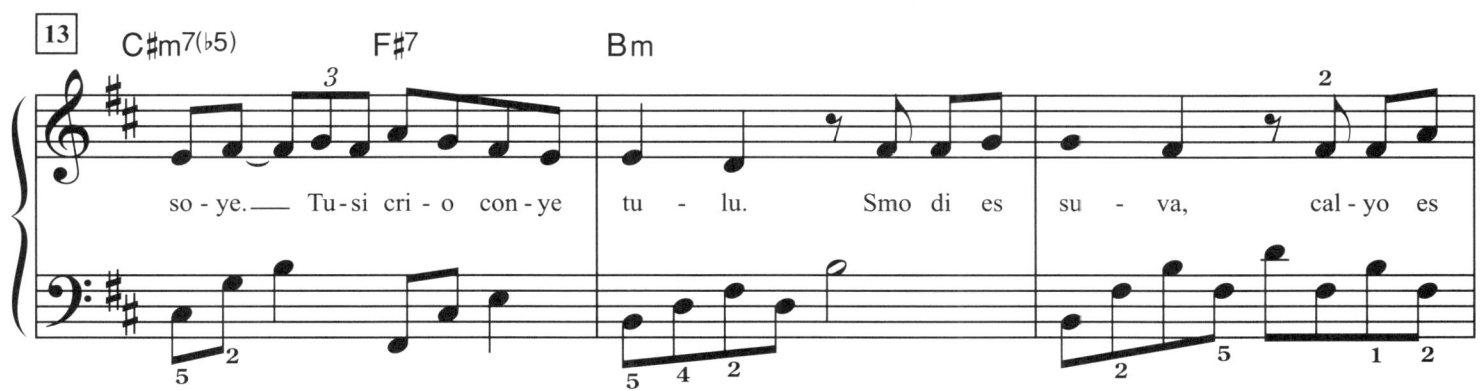
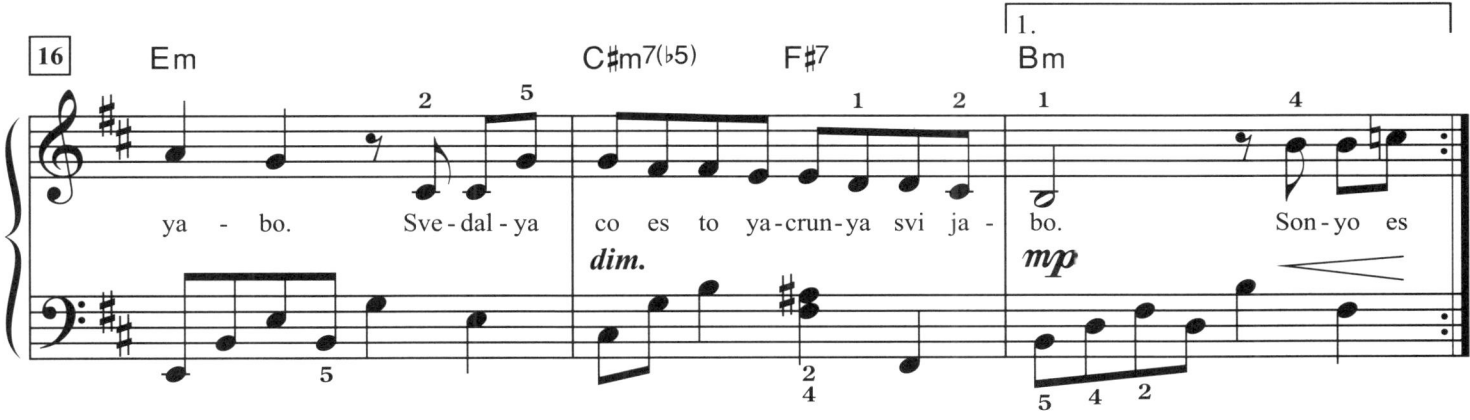

LET ME FALL
(from "Quidam")

Music by Benoit Jutras
Lyrics by Jim Corcoran
Arranged by Dan Coates

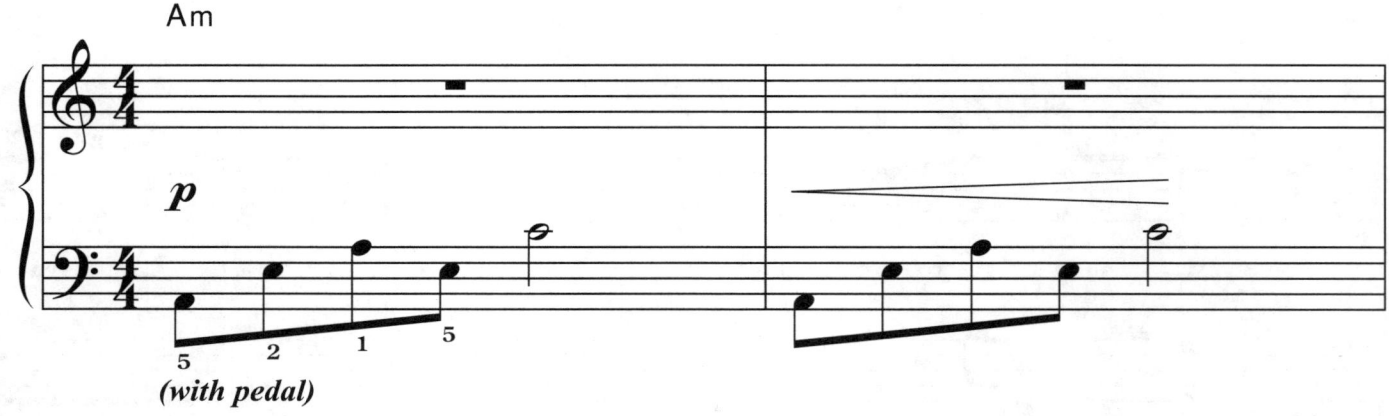

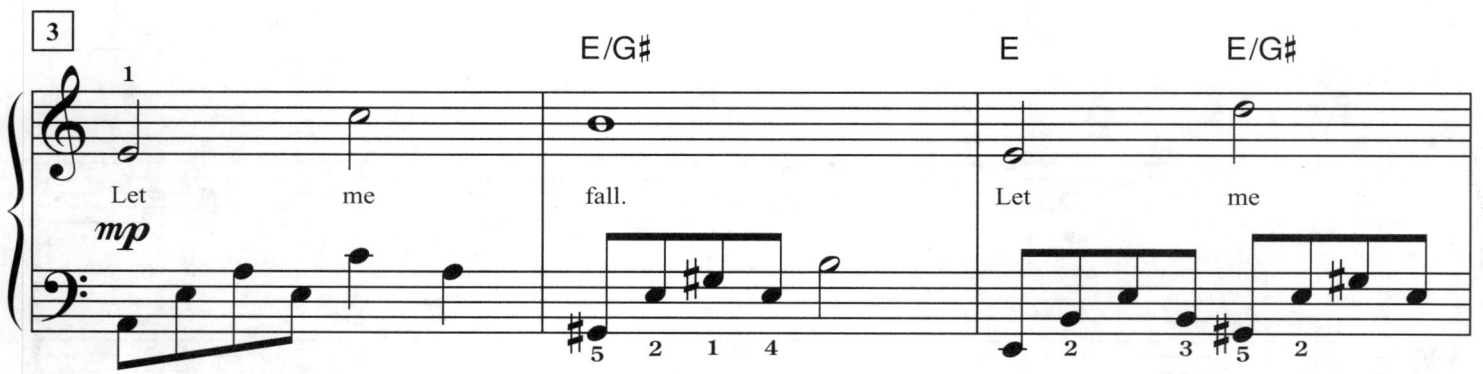

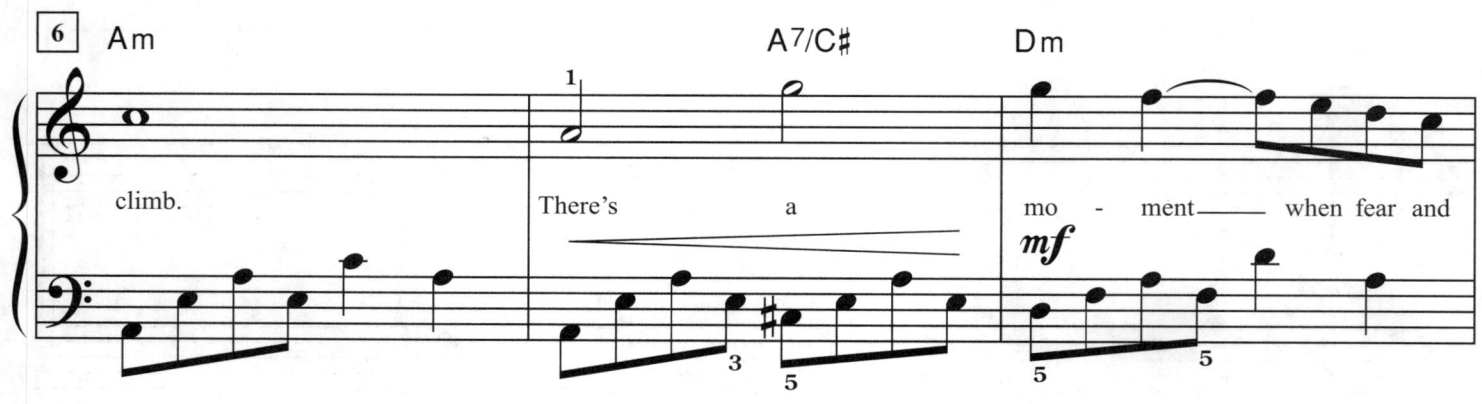

© 1996 CRÉATIONS MÉANDRES INC. and LES ÉDITIONS GOG ET MAGOG INC.
All Rights Reserved

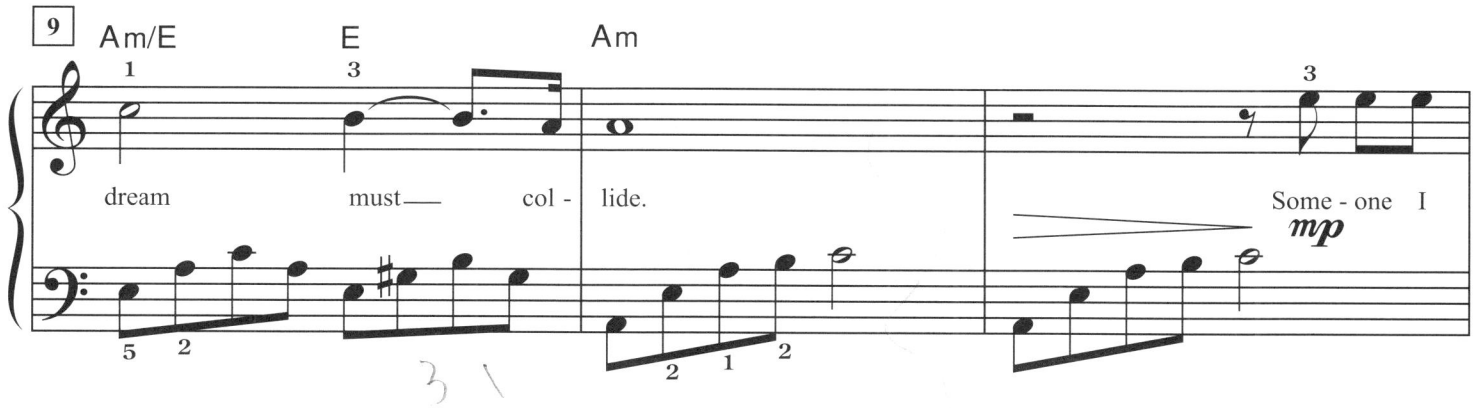
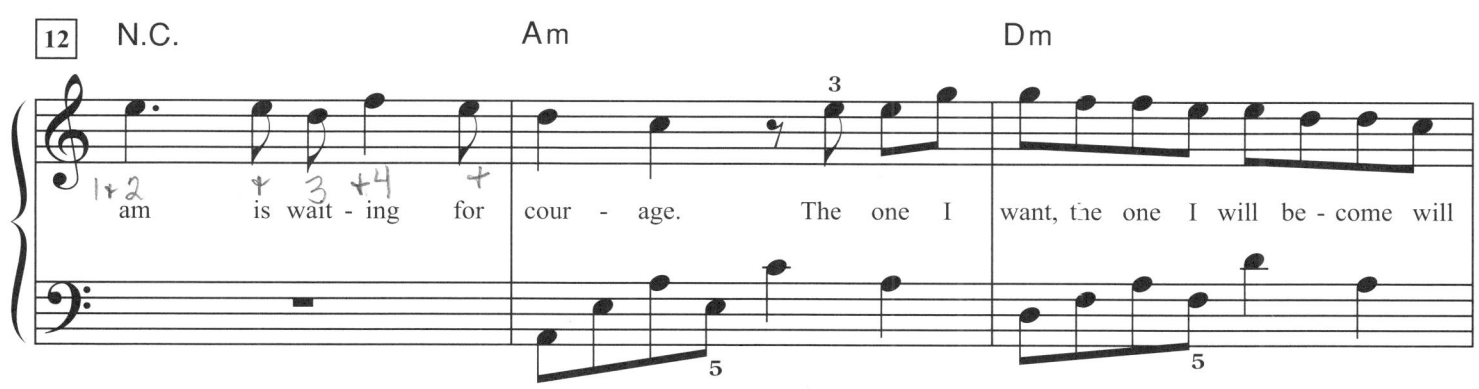
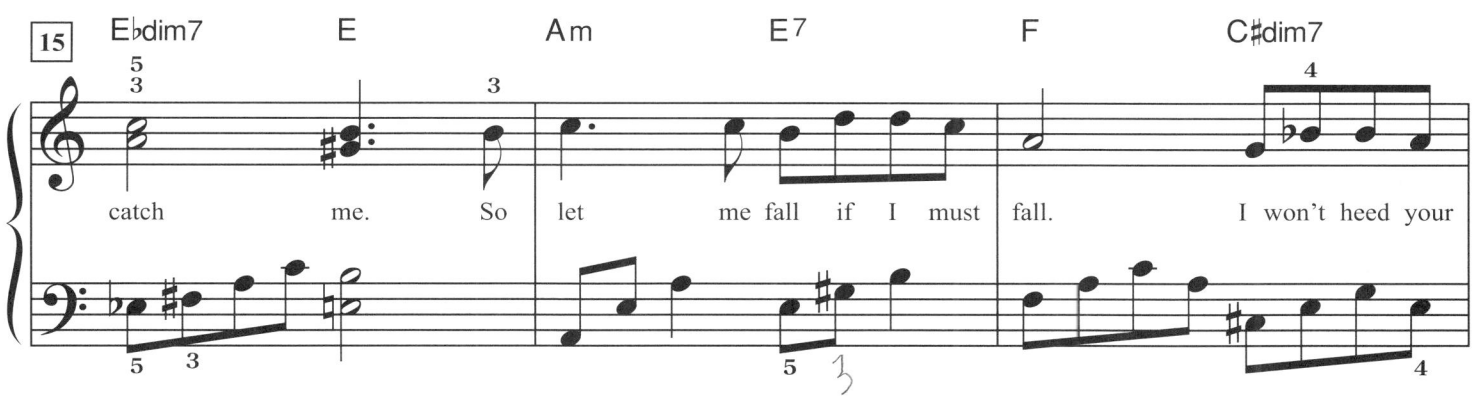
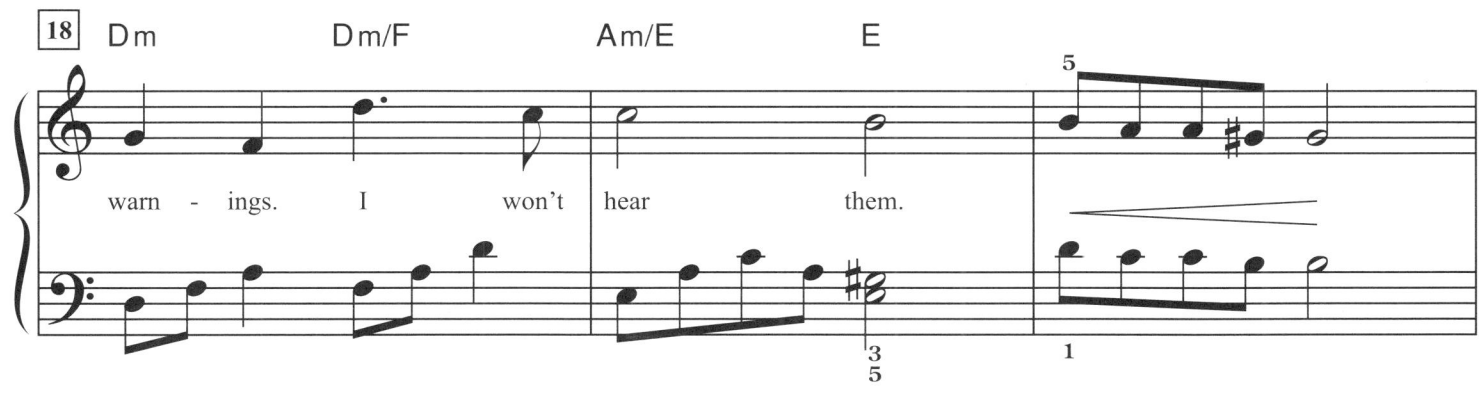

40

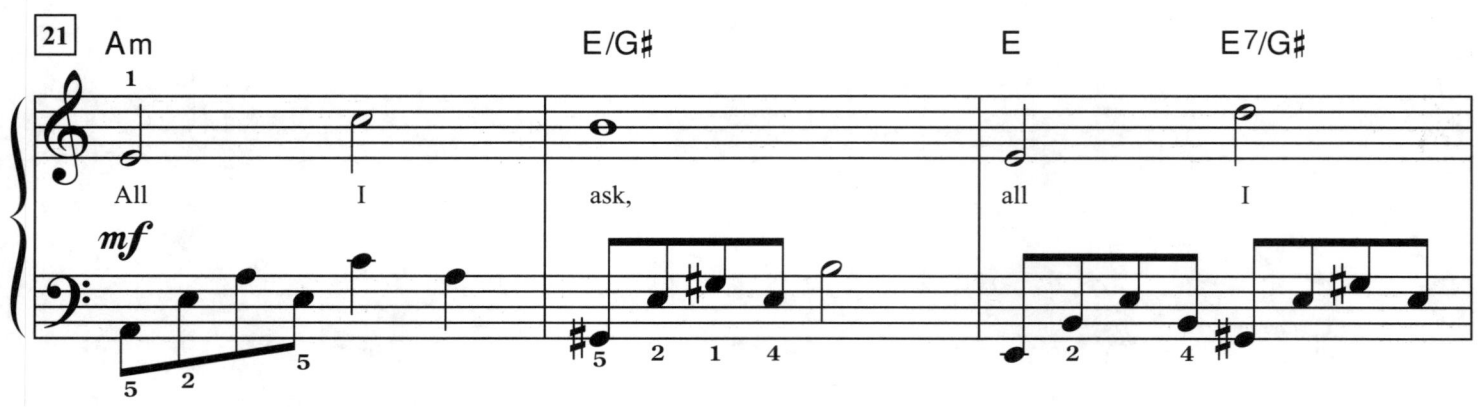
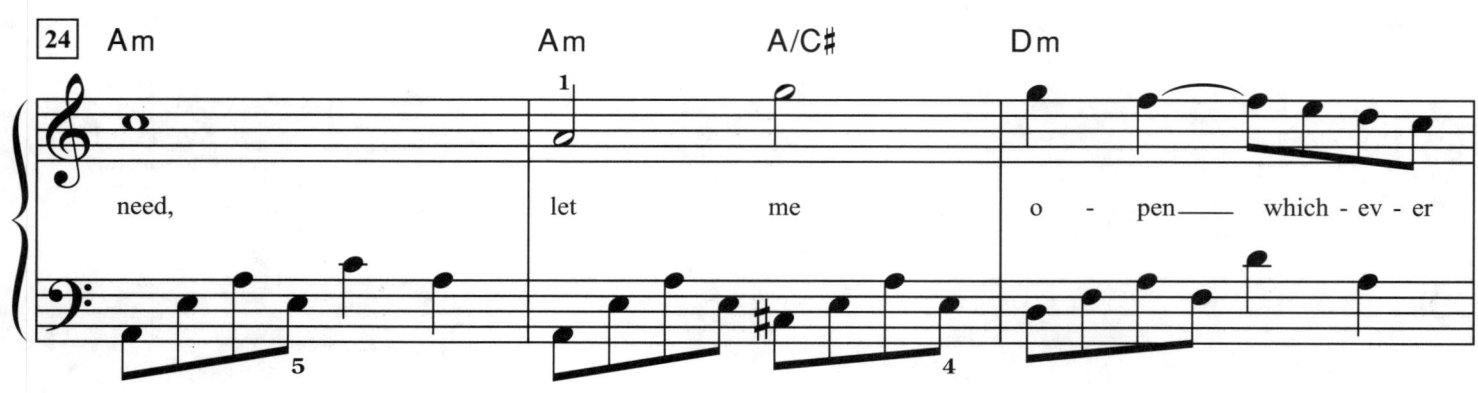
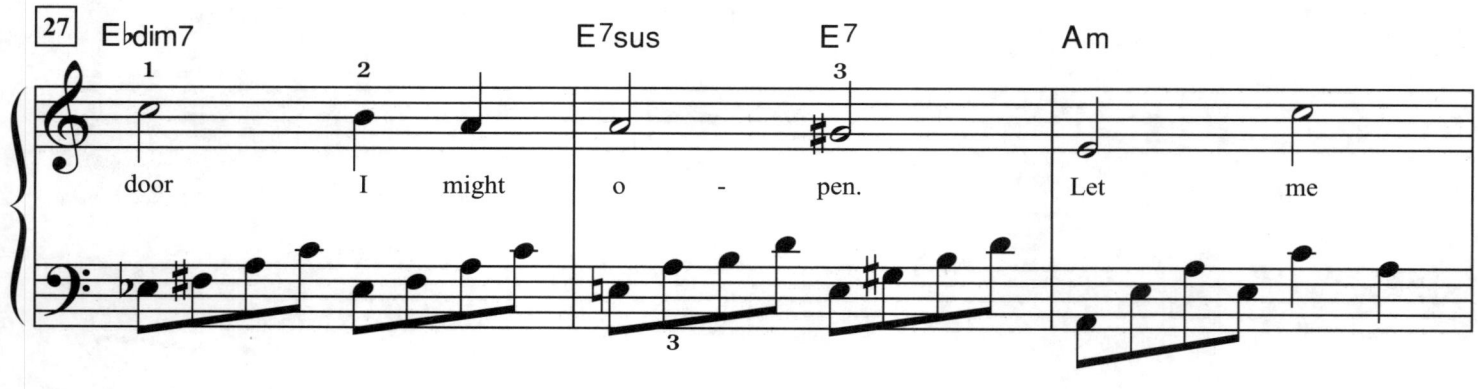

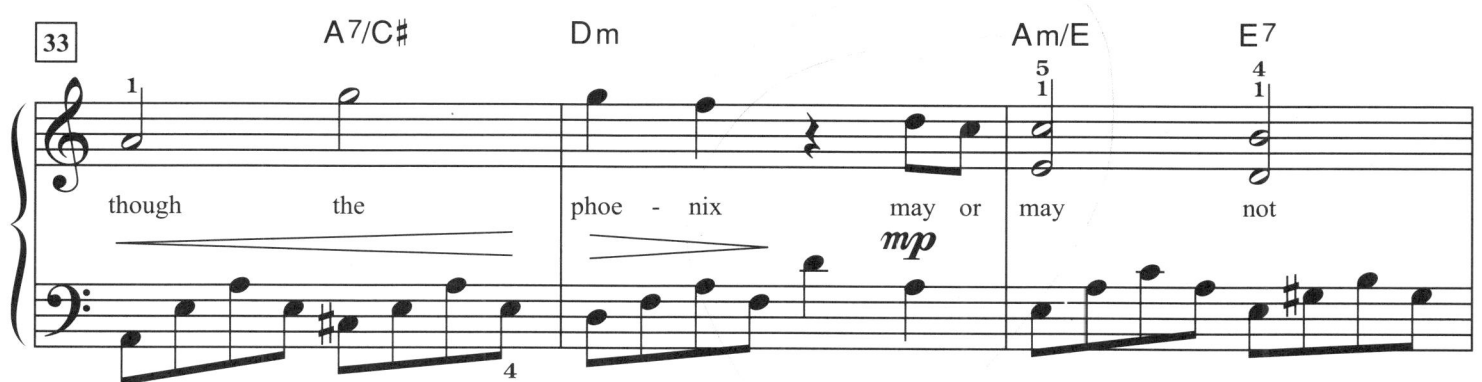
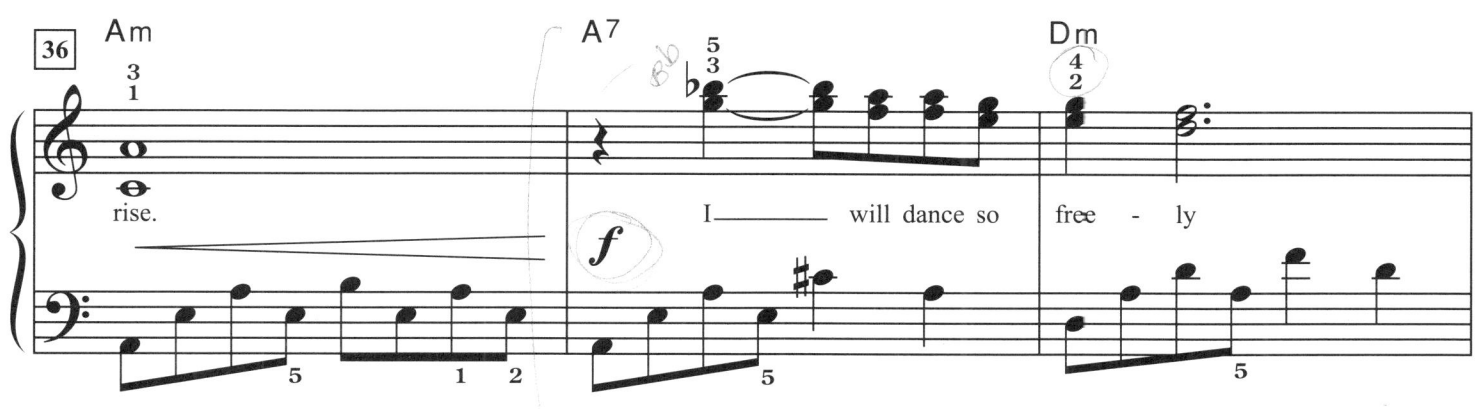
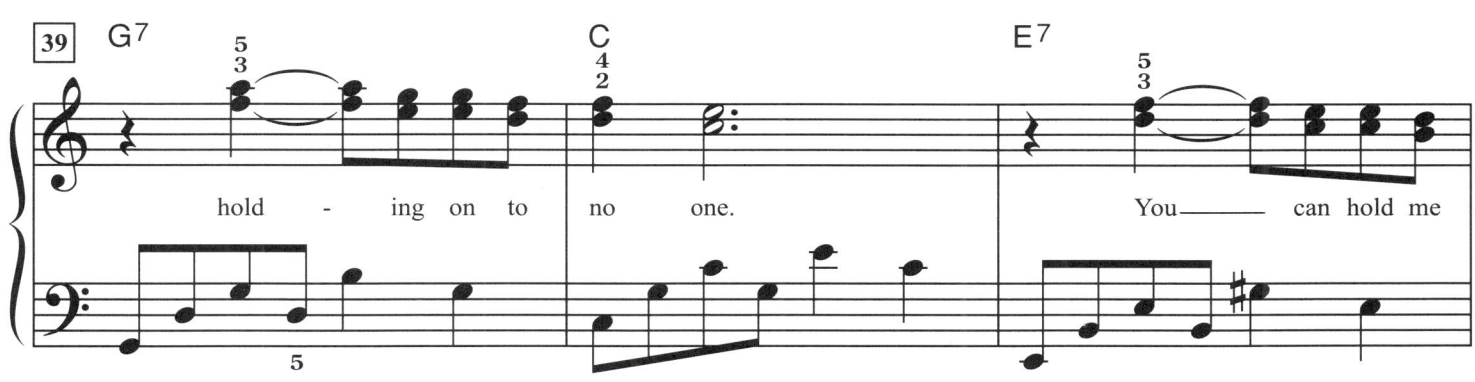

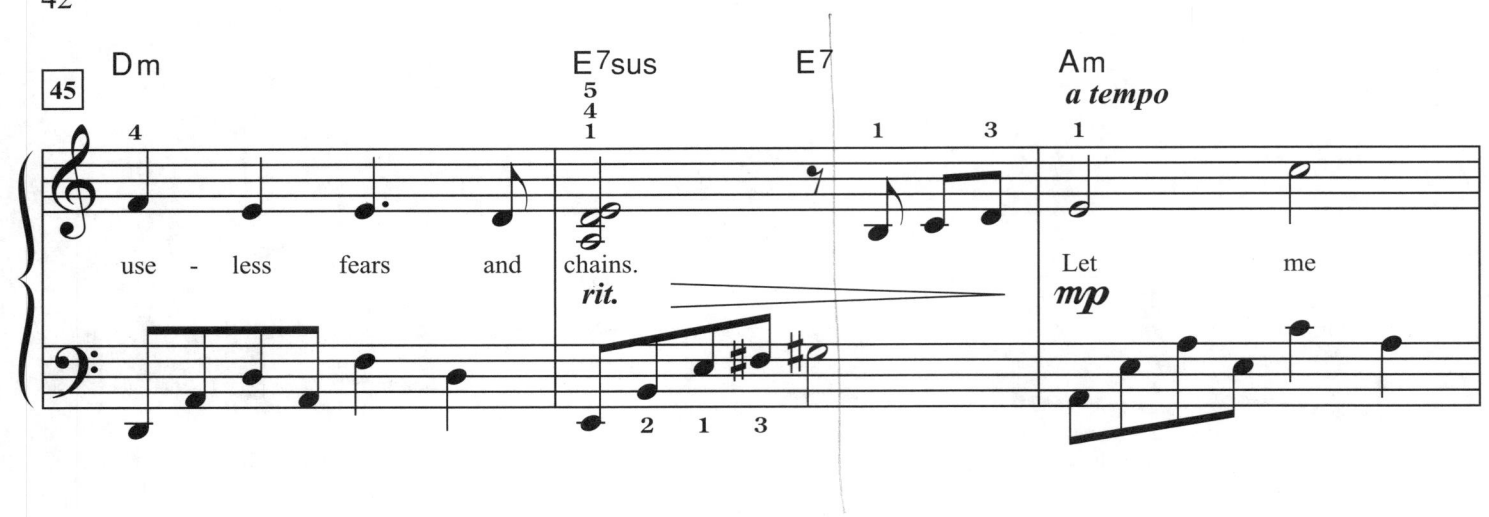
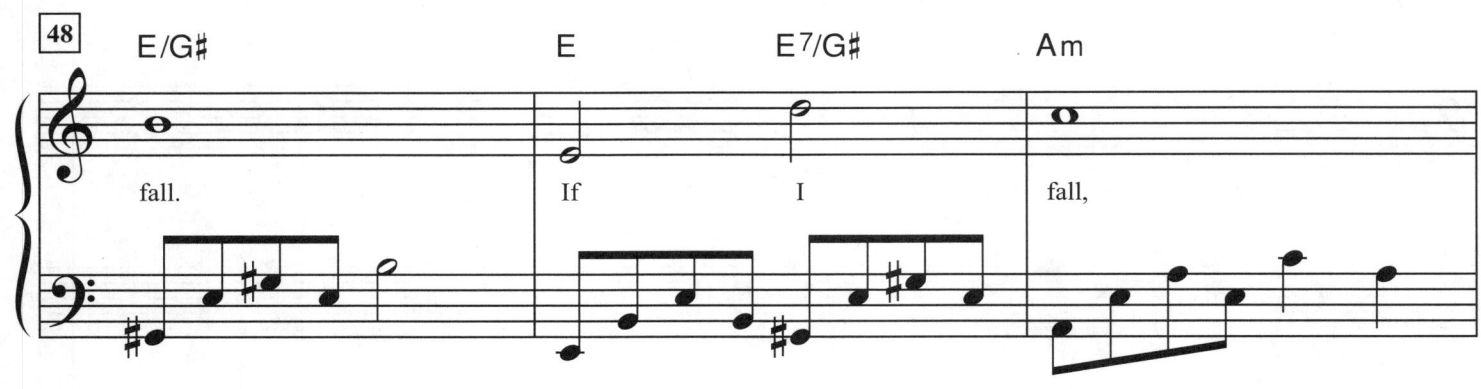
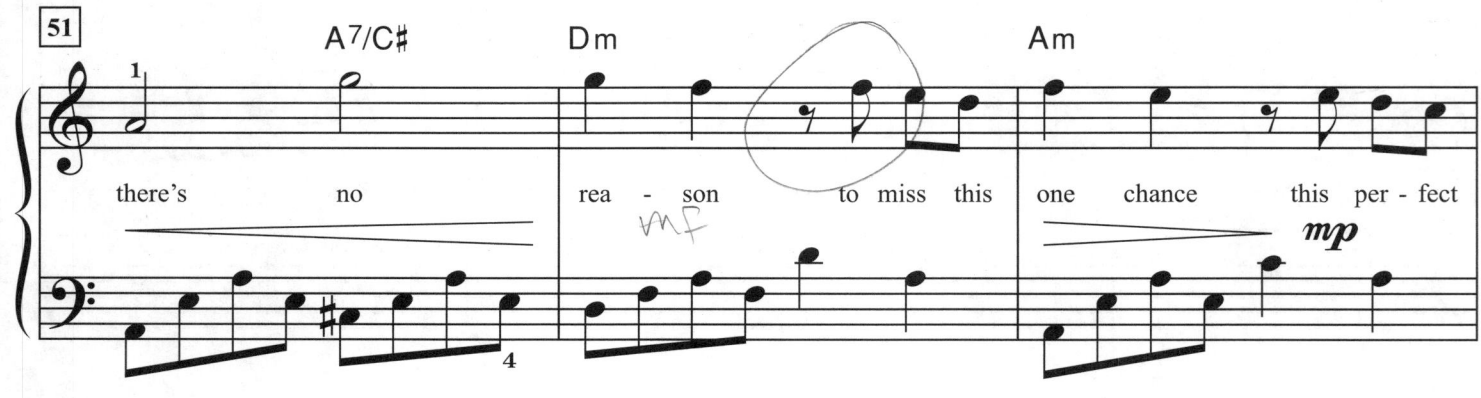

O
(from "O")

Composed by Benoit Jutras
Arranged by Dan Coates

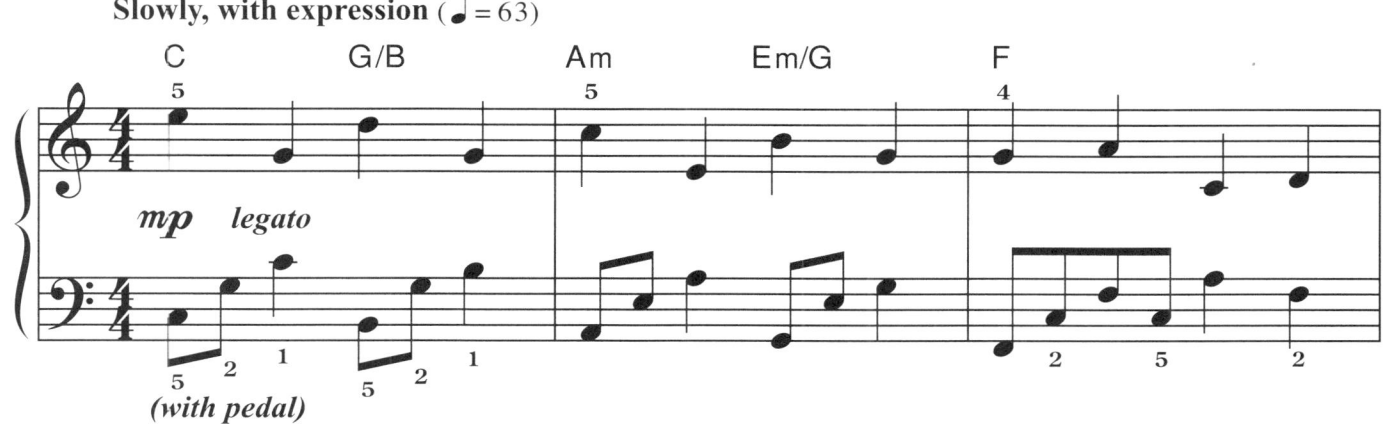

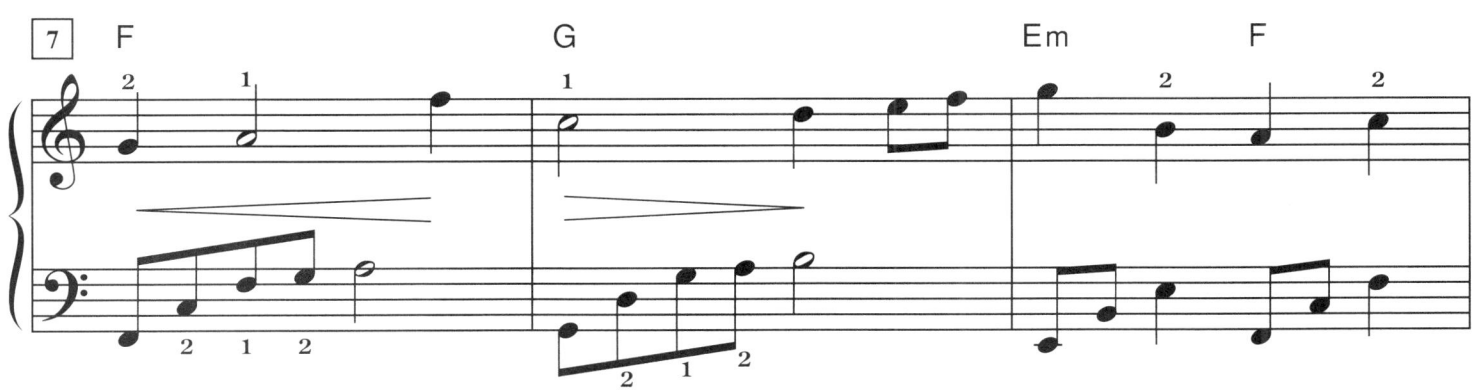

© 1998 CRÉATIONS MÉANDRES INC.
All Rights Reserved

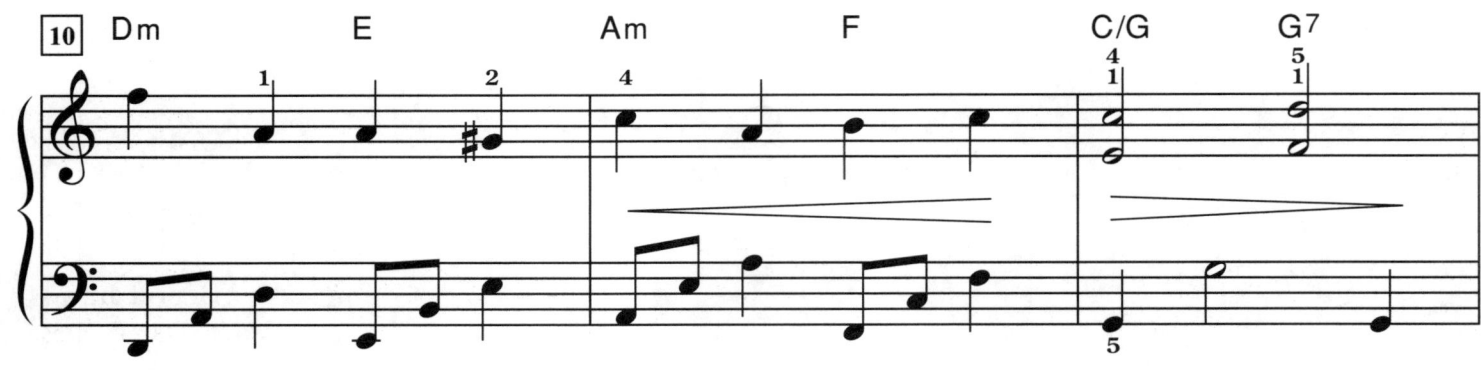

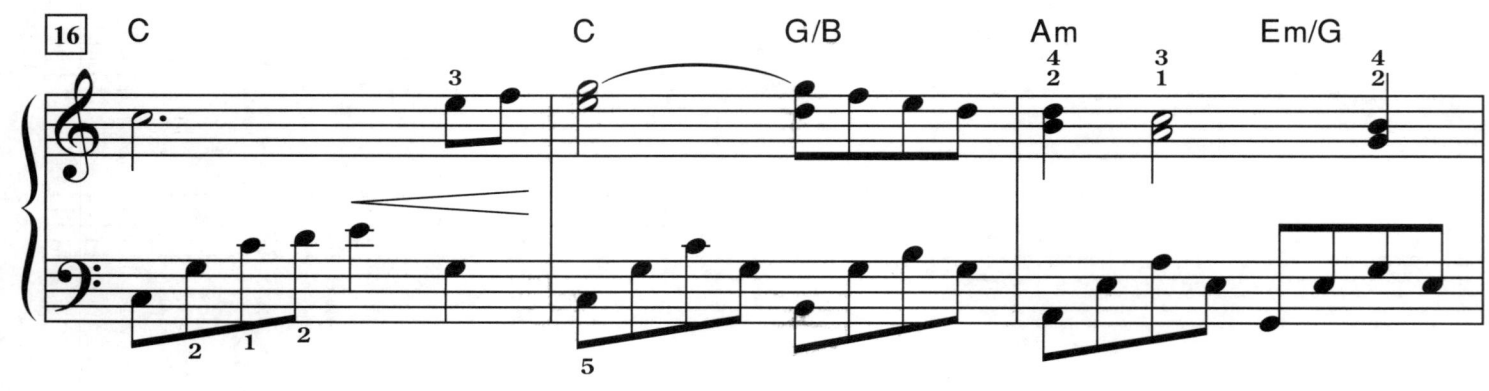
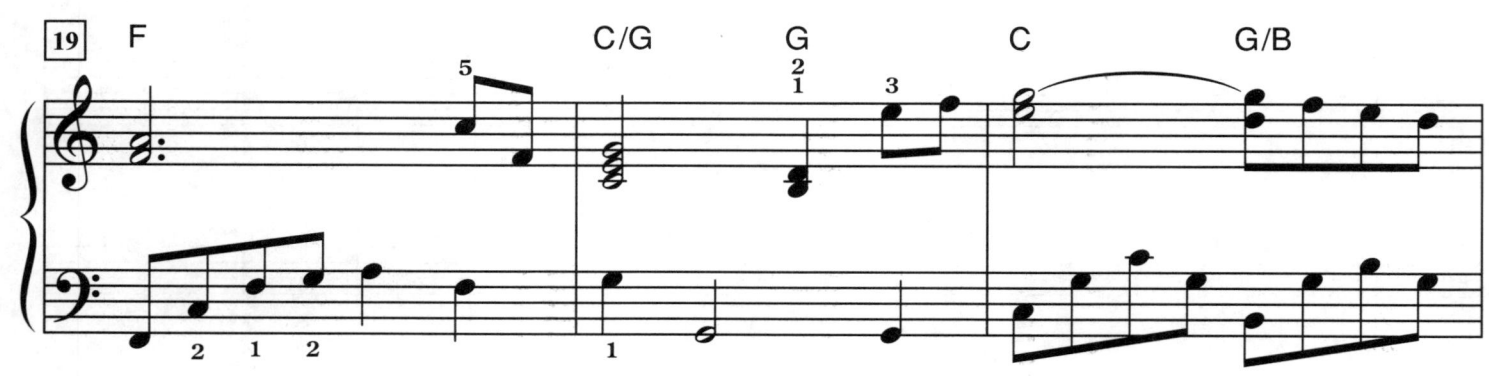

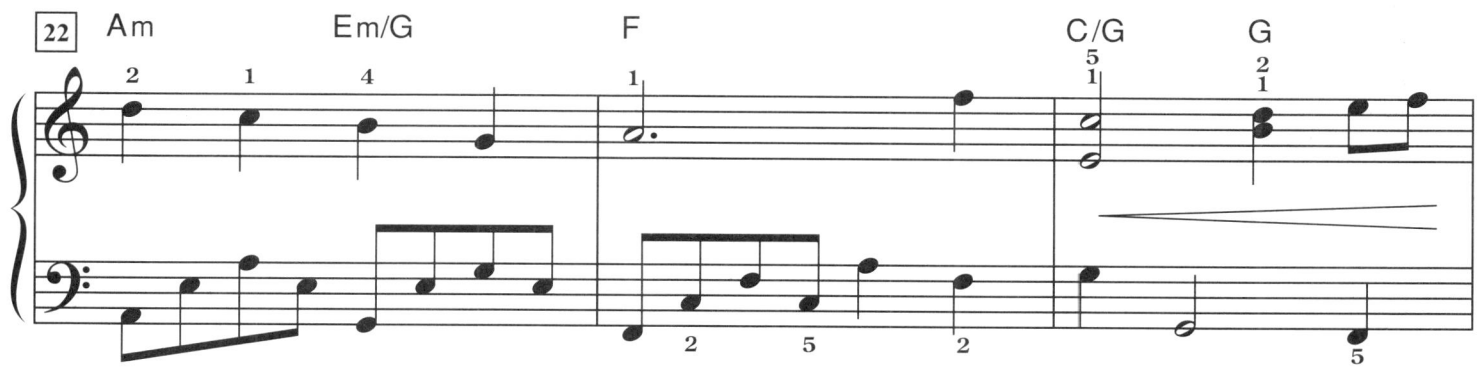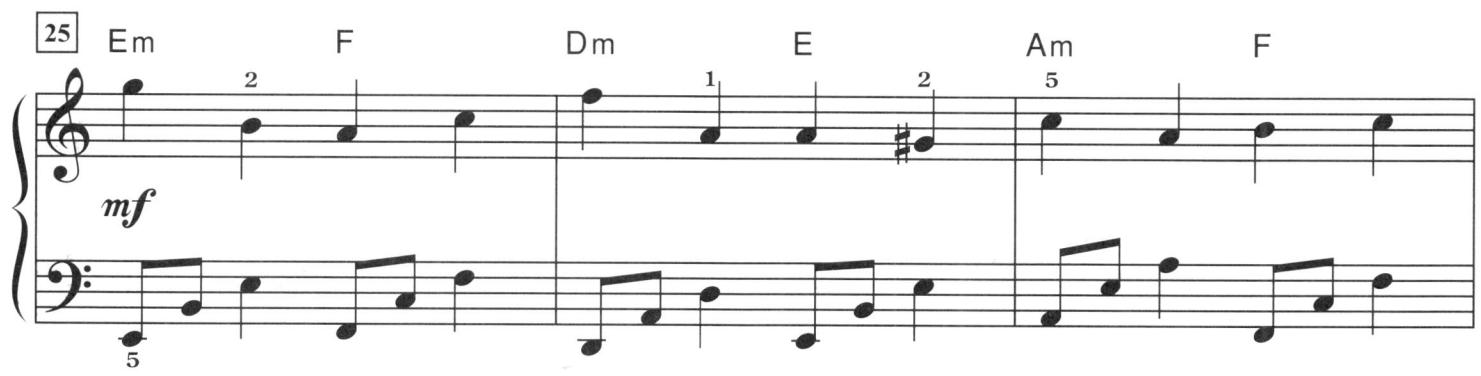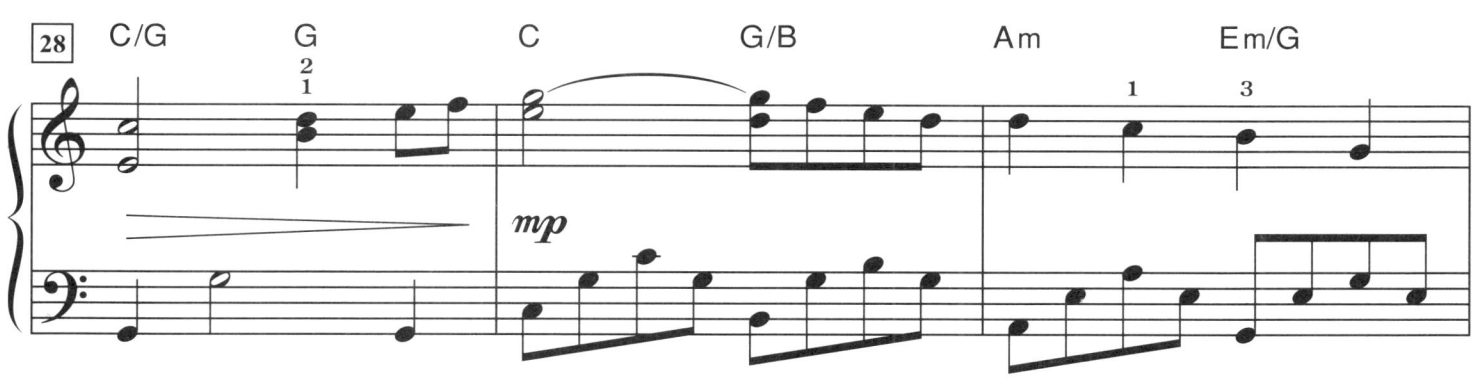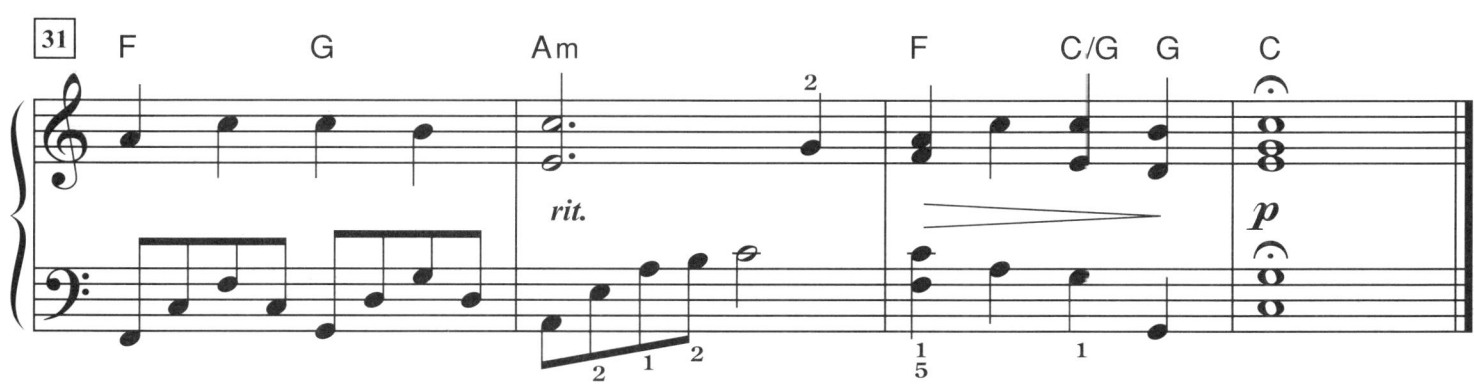

PAGEANT
(from "KÀ")

Composed by René Dupéré
Arranged by Dan Coates

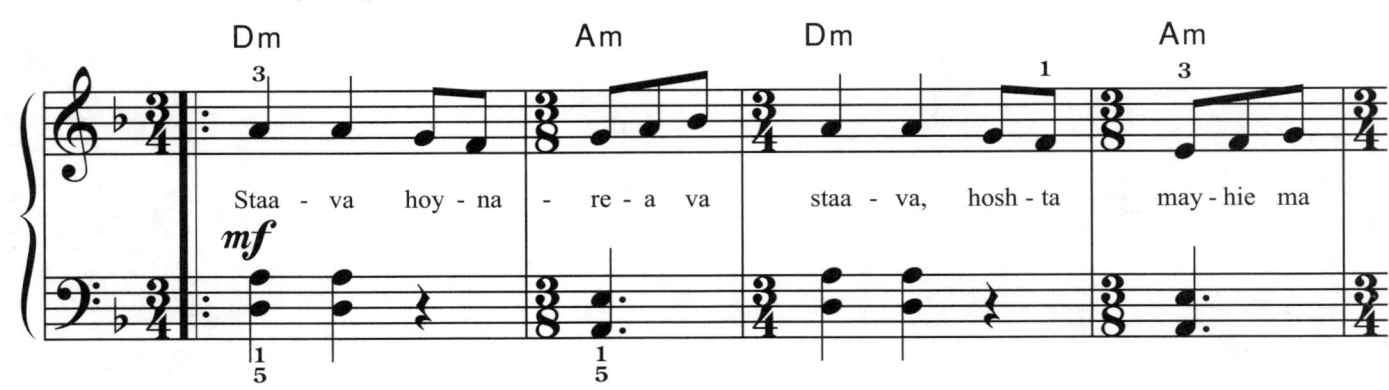
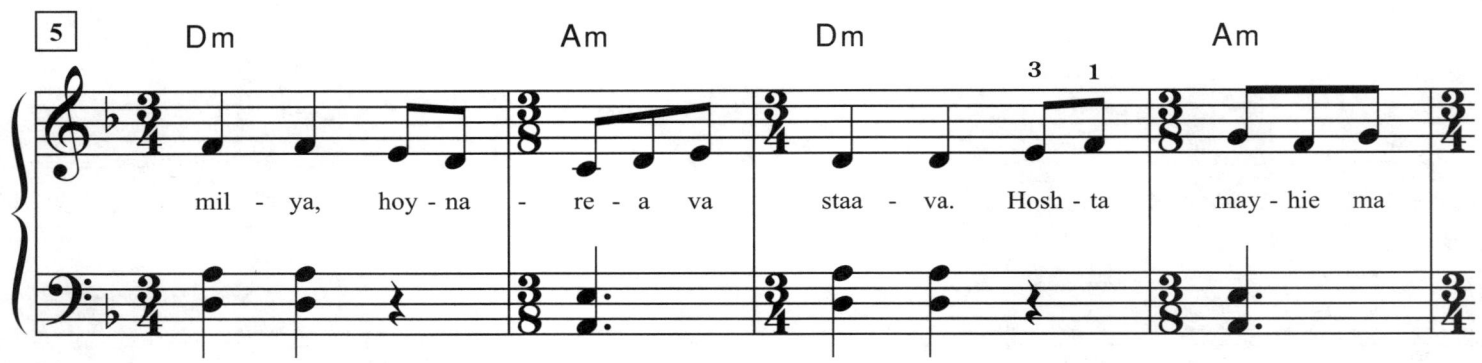
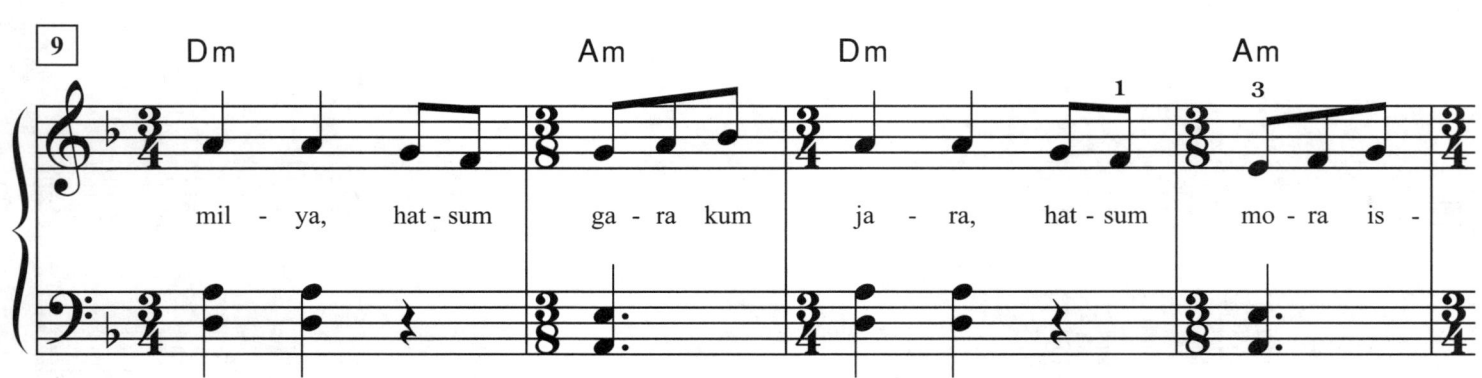

© 2005 CRÉATIONS MÉANDRES INC.
All Rights Reserved

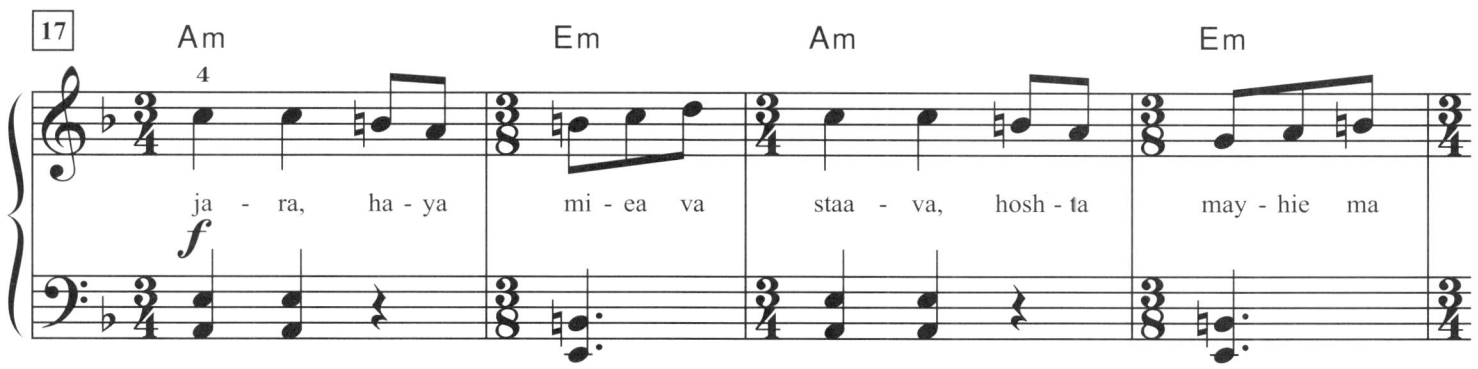
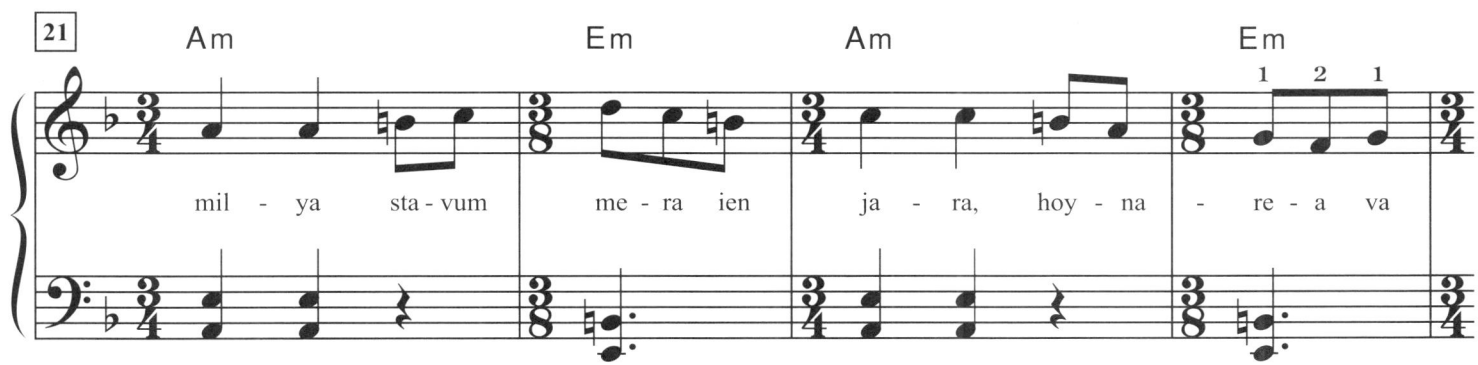

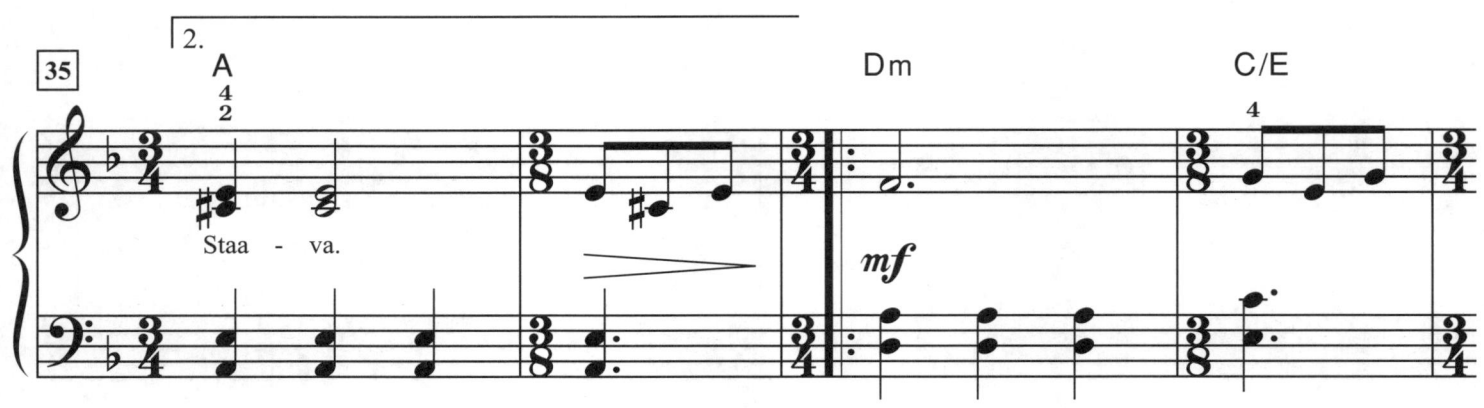
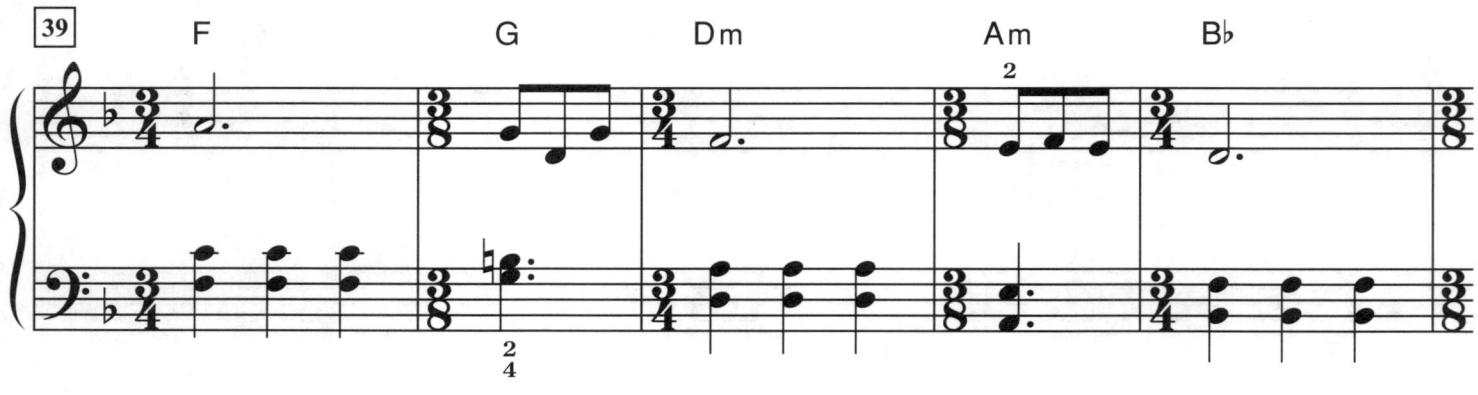
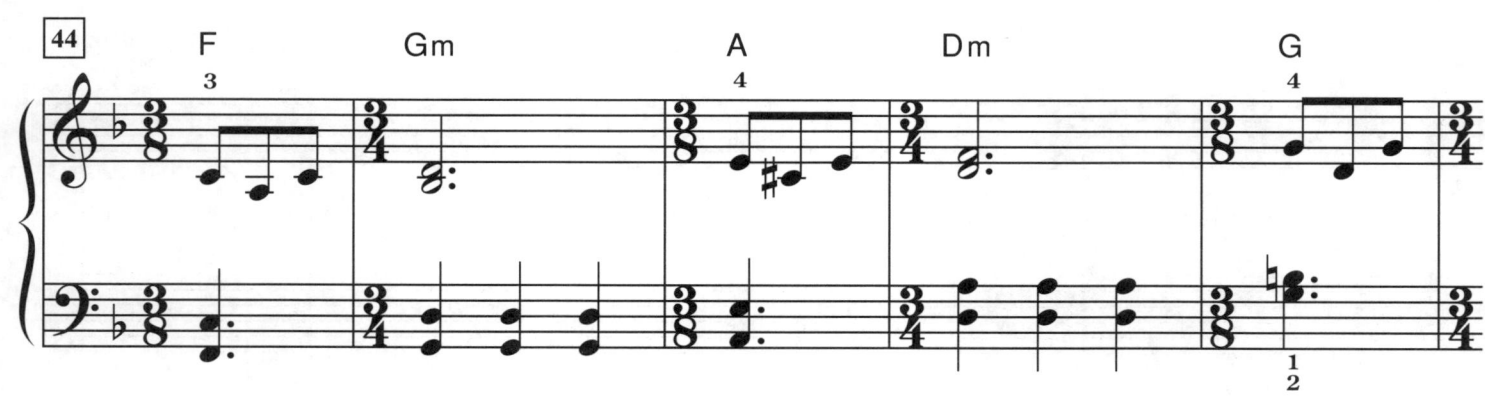

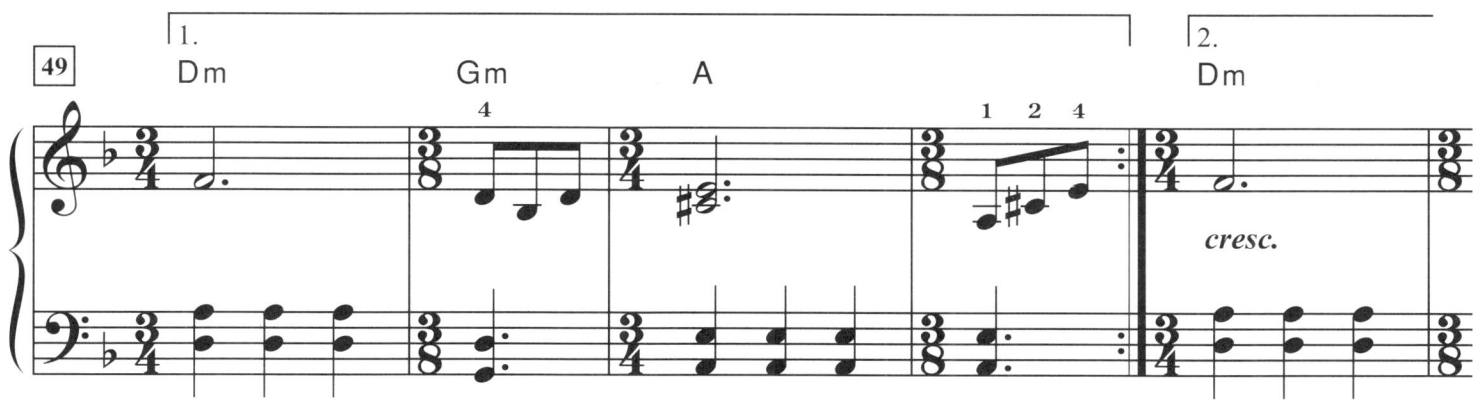
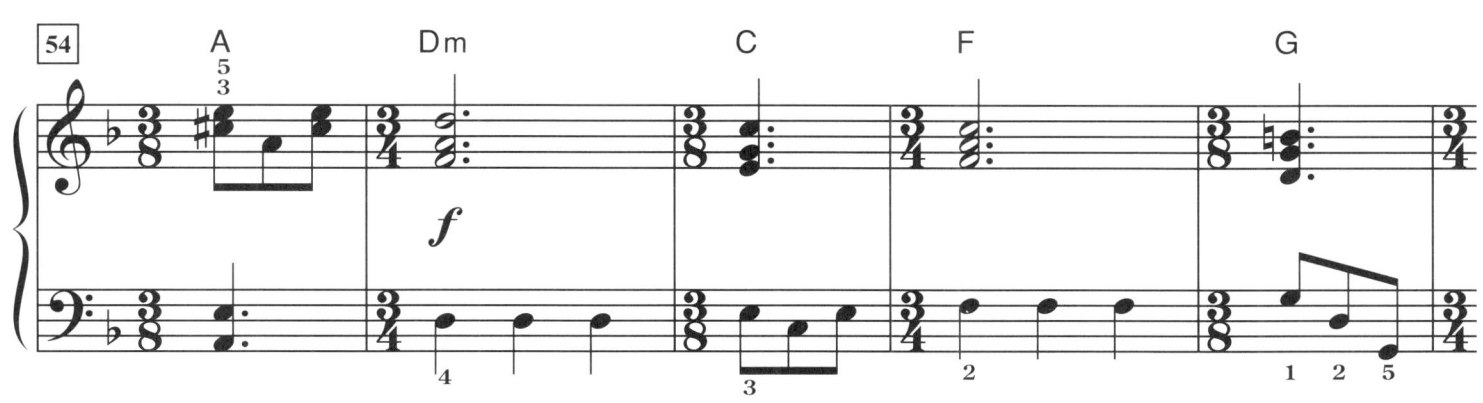

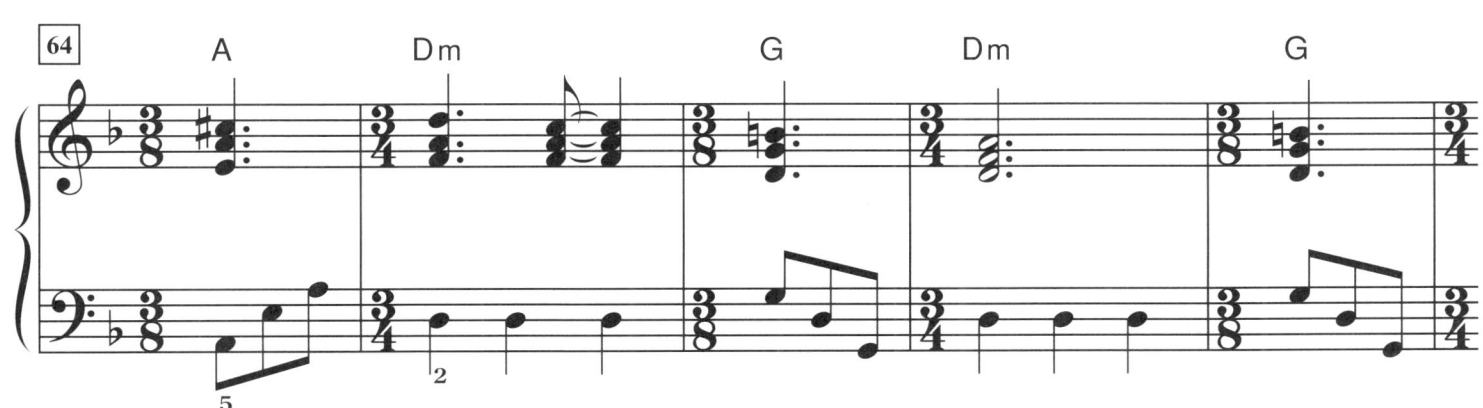

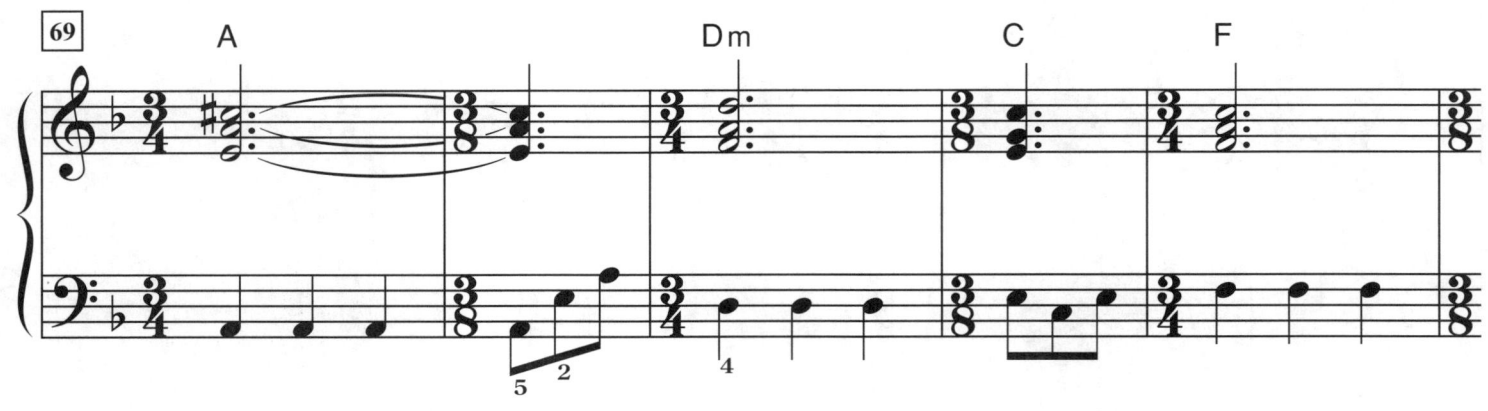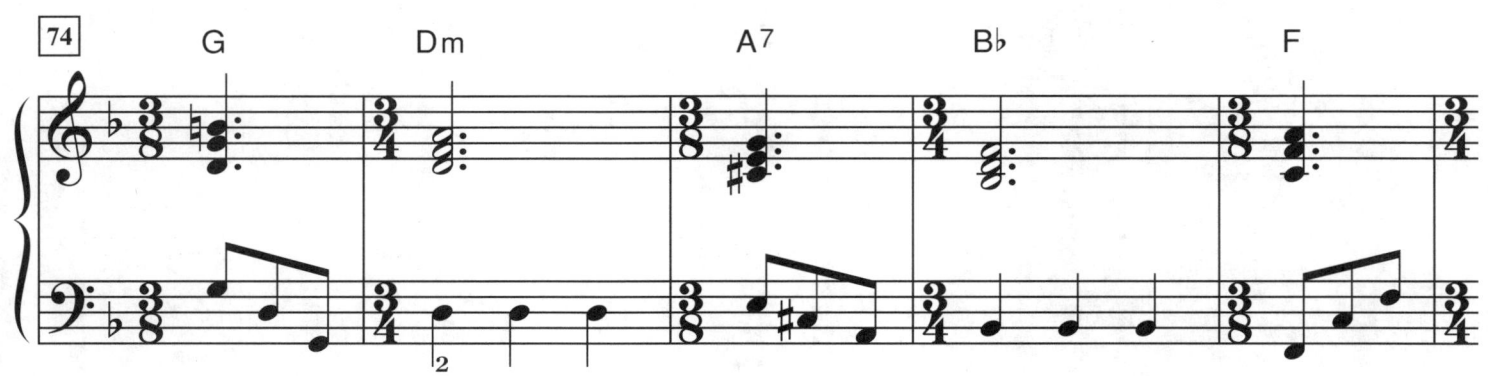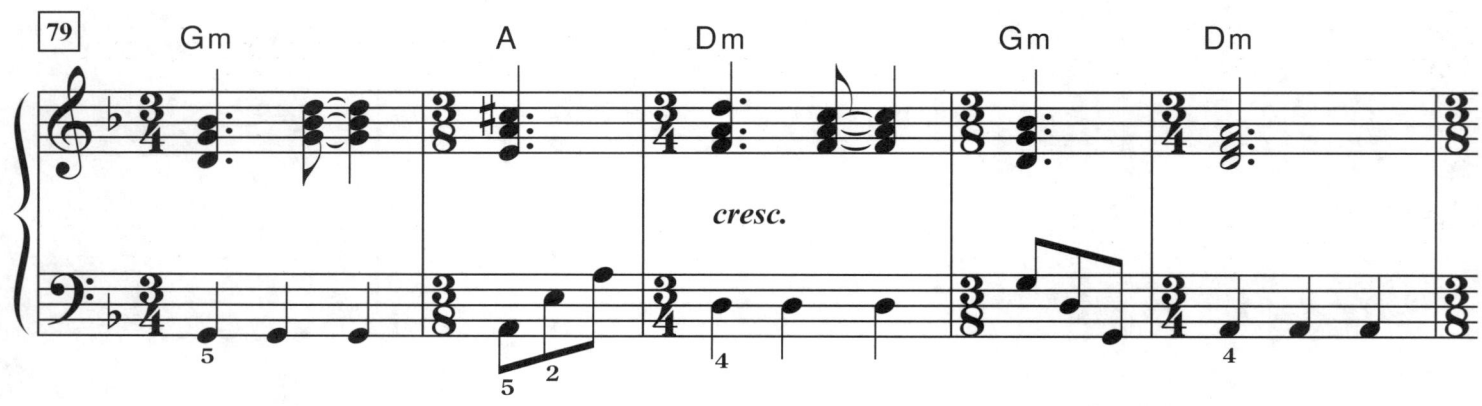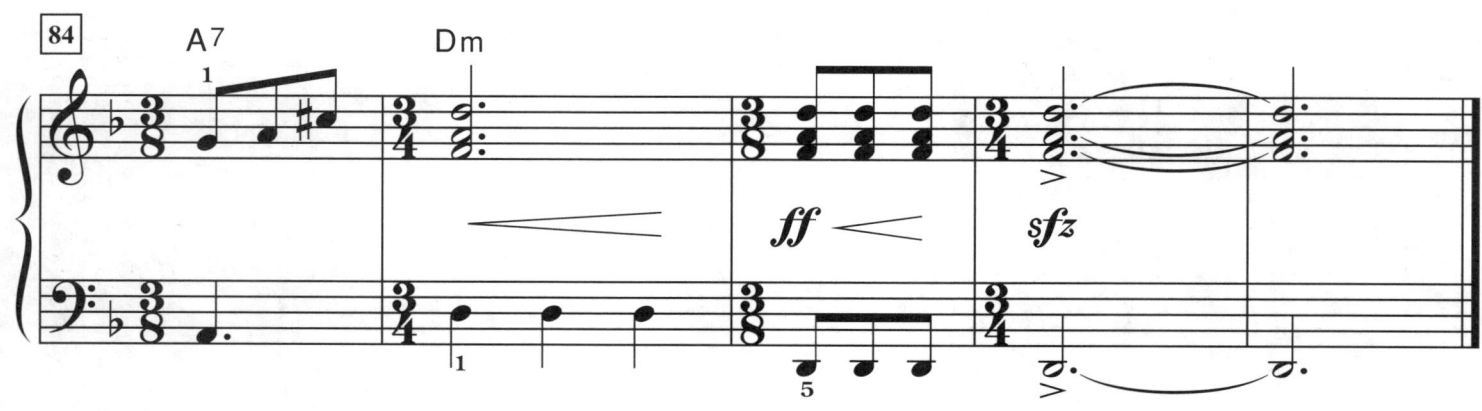

QUIDAM
(from "Quidam")

Music by Benoit Jutras
Lyrics by Jim Corcoran
Arranged by Dan Coates

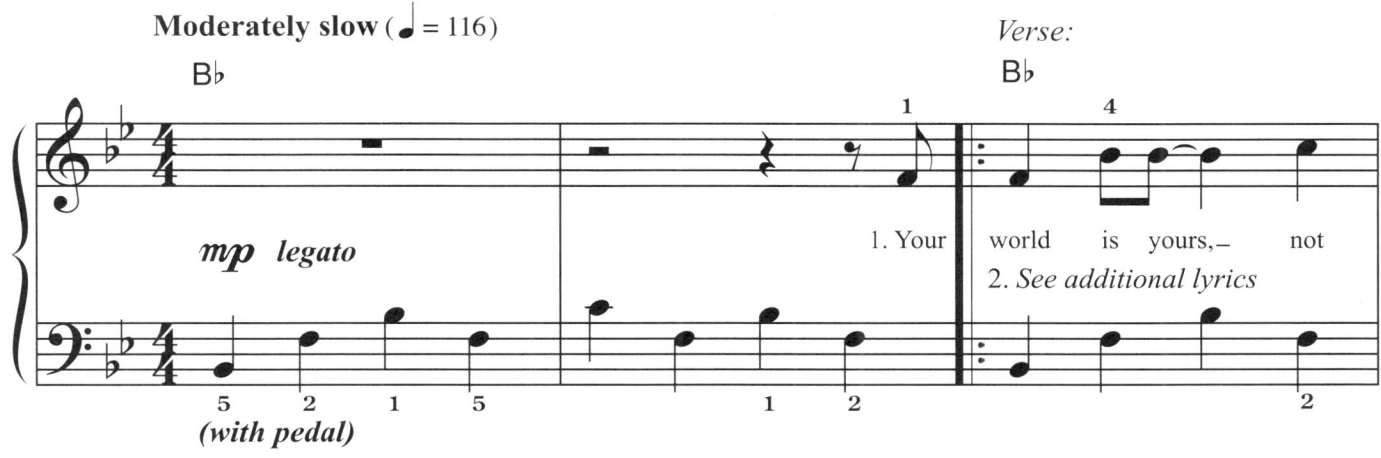

© 1996 CRÉATIONS MÉANDRES INC. and LES ÉDITIONS GOG ET MAGOG
All Rights Reserved

52

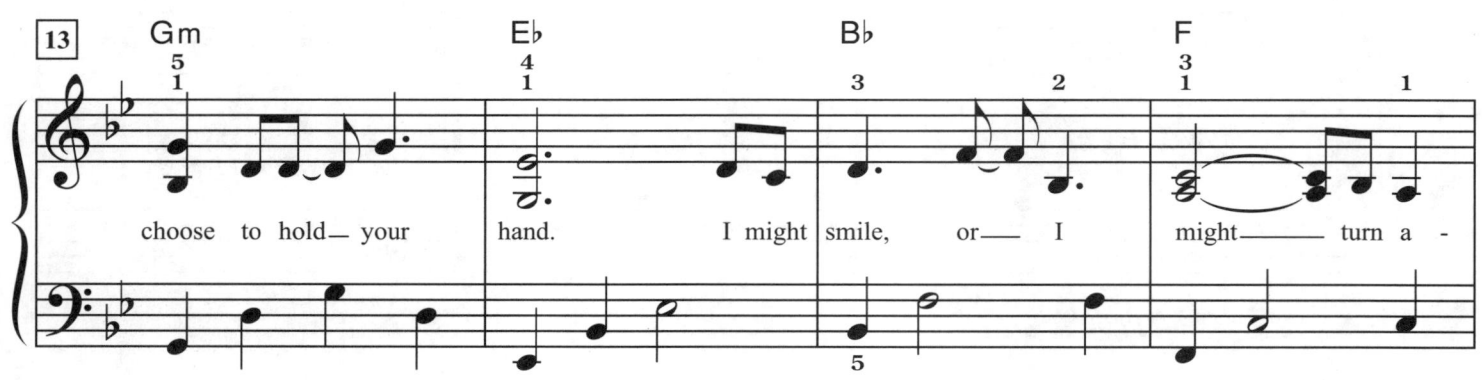

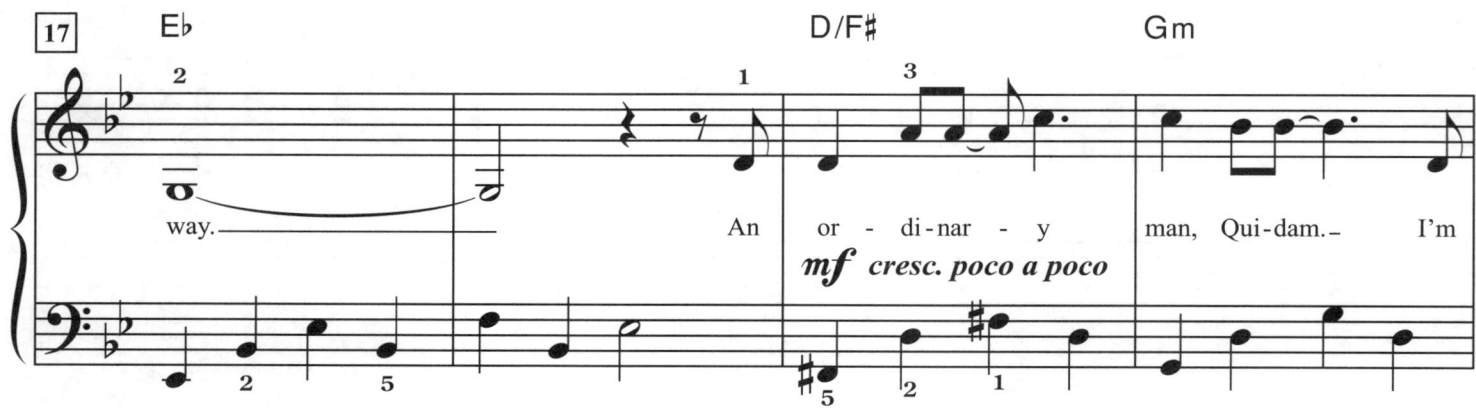

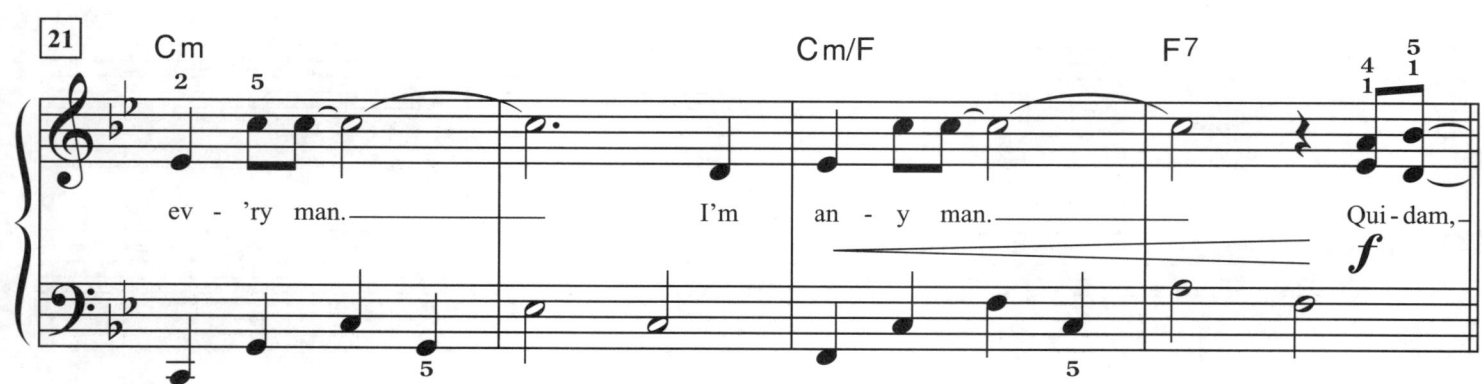

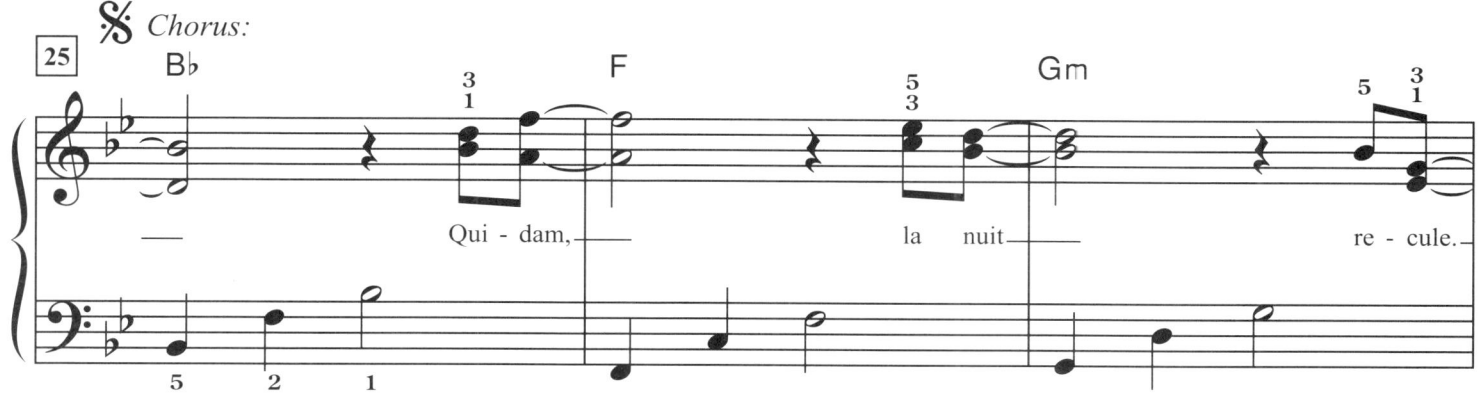

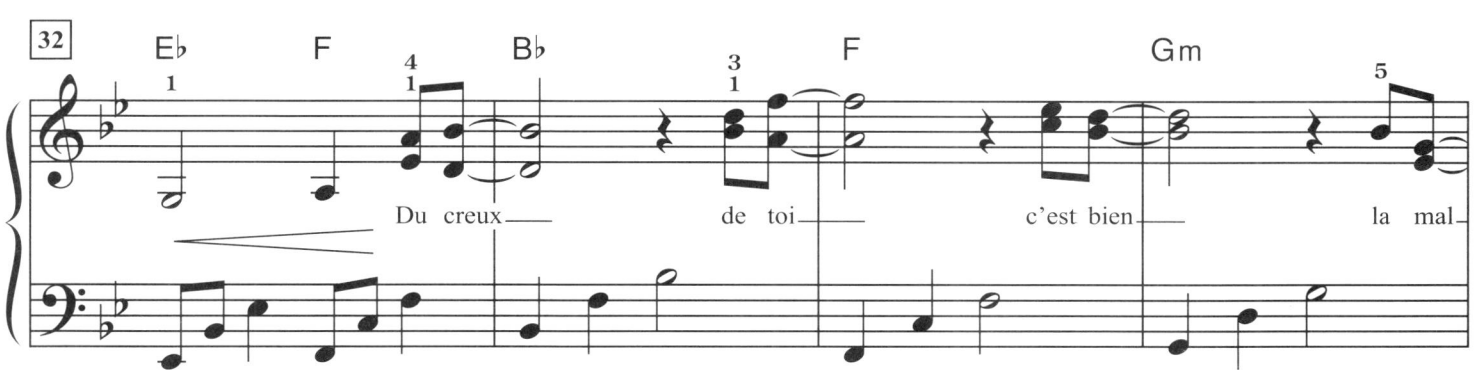

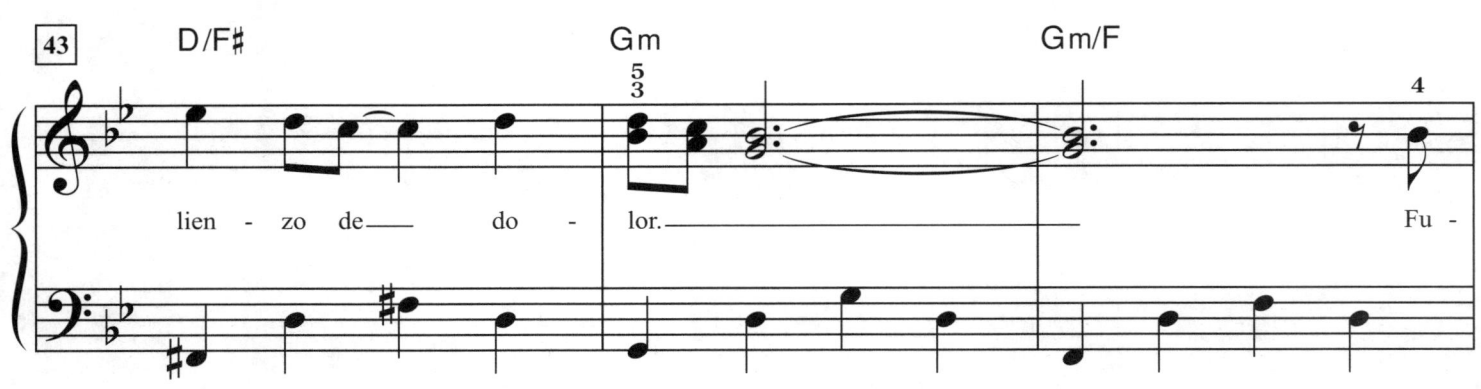
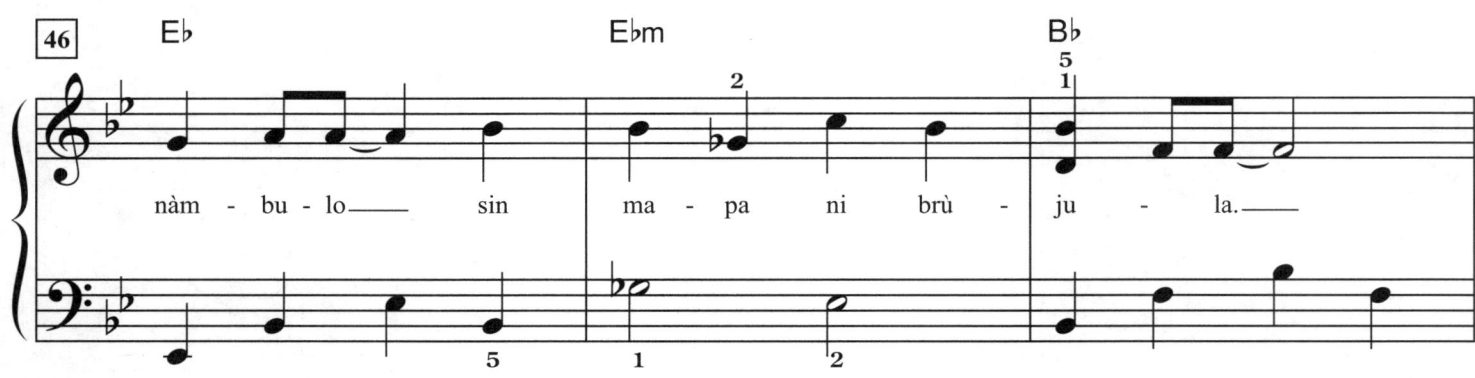
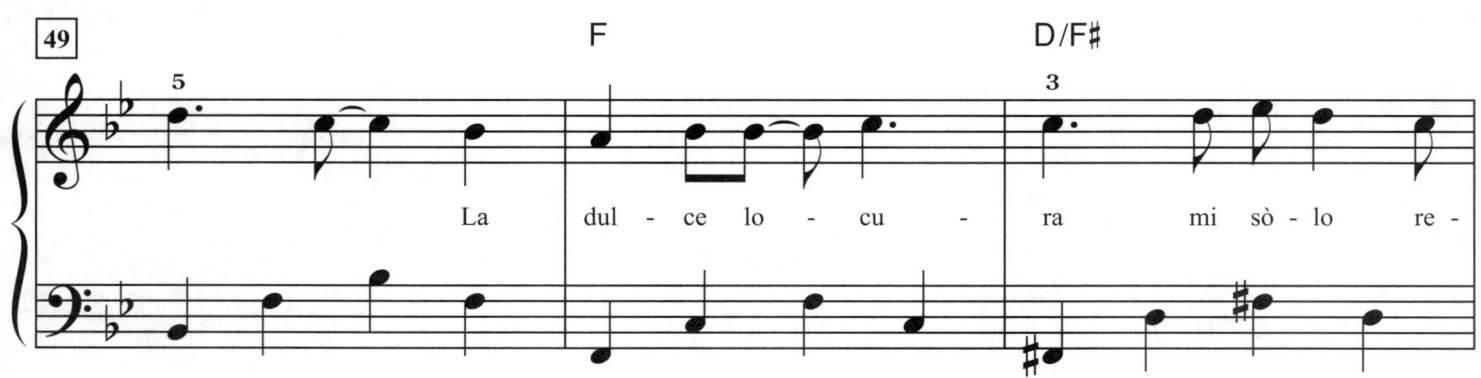

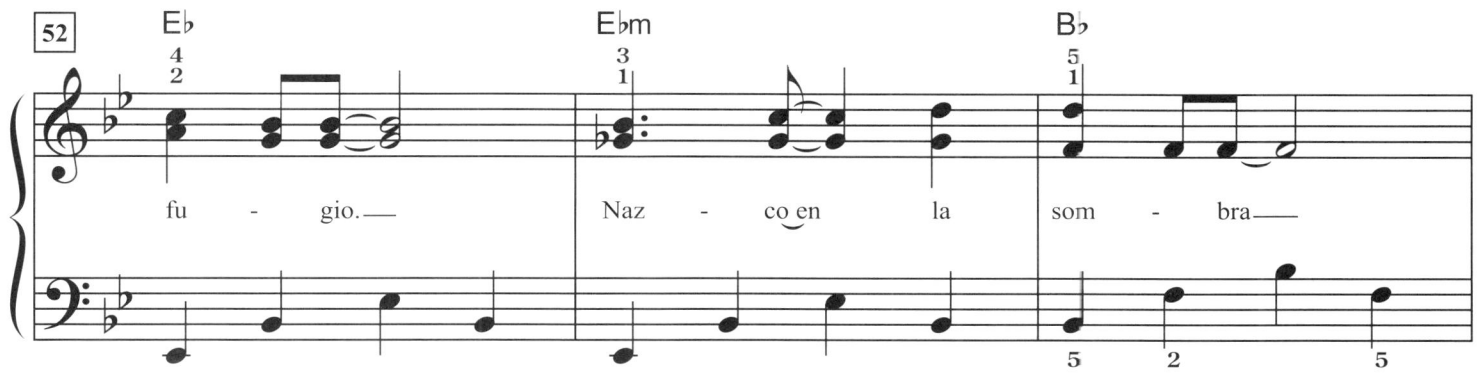

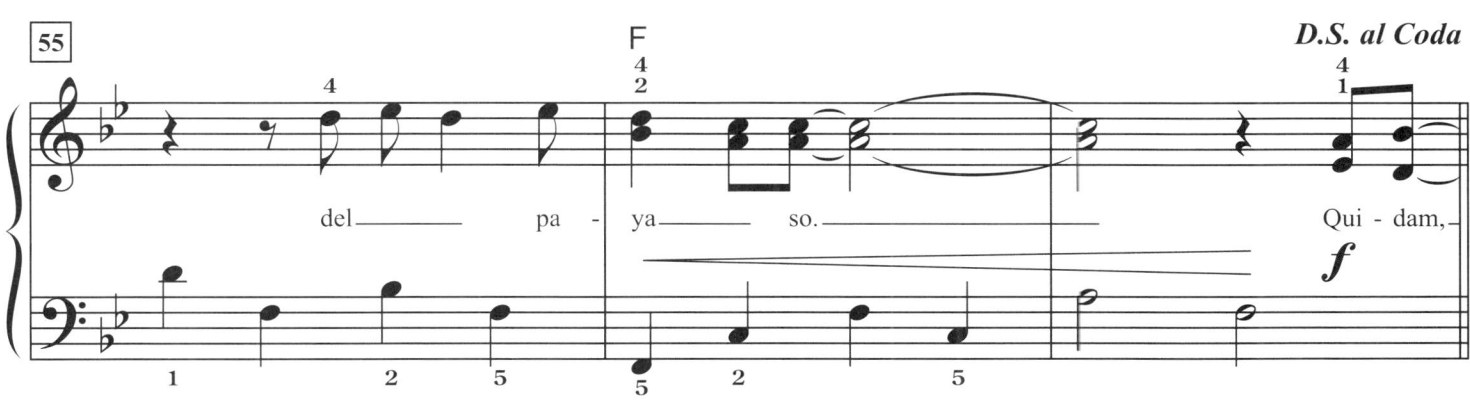

Verse 2:
There's nothing left, there's nothing right,
There's nothing wrong.
I'm one, I'm two, I'm all yet none of you.
The truth, the lie, the tear, the laughter,
The hand and the empty touch.
Here I am alone, waiting for the curtain call.
An ordinary man, Quidam.
I'm every man.
I'm any man.
(To Chorus:)

TRIANGLE TANGO
(from "Corteo")

Music by Philippe Leduc
Arranged by Dan Coates

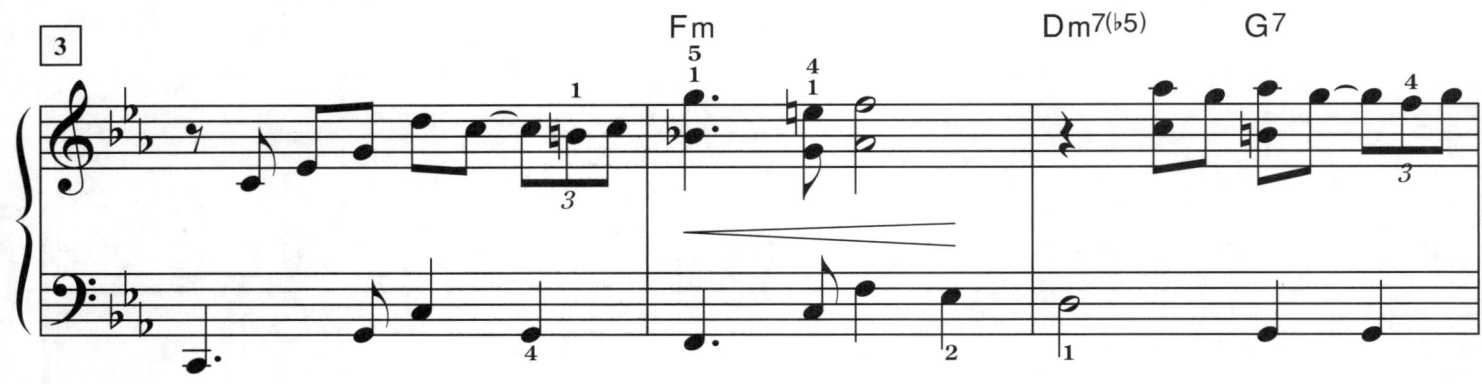

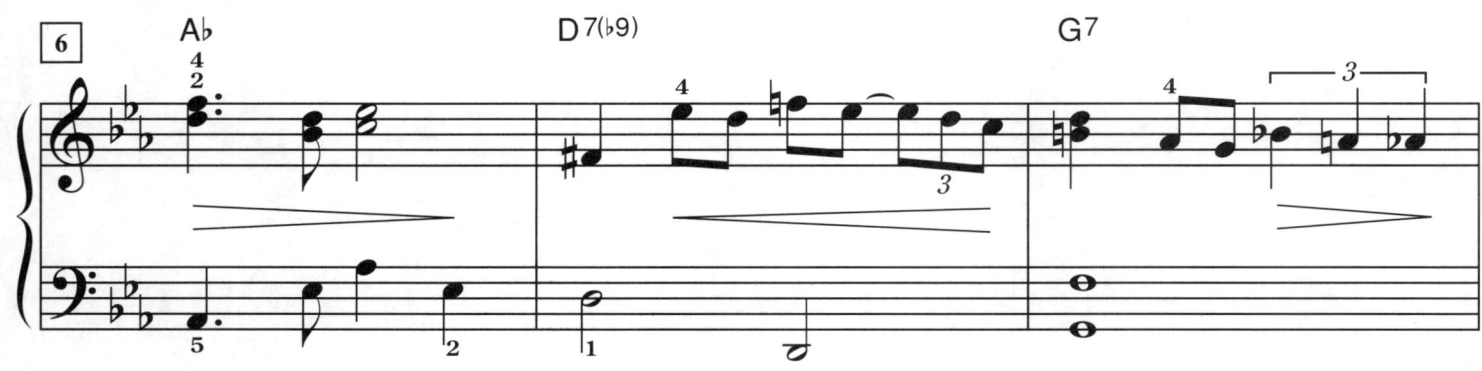

© 2005 CRÉATIONS MÉANDRES INC.
All Rights Reserved

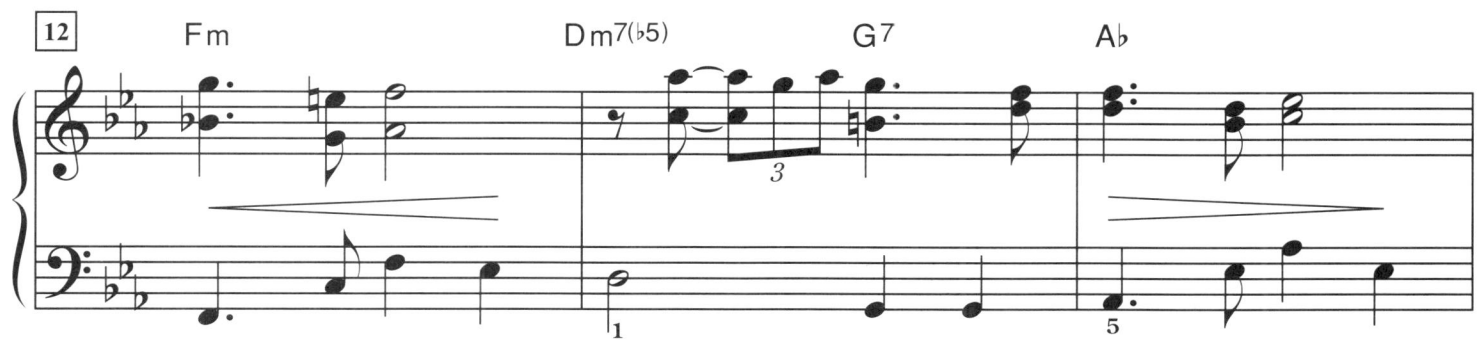
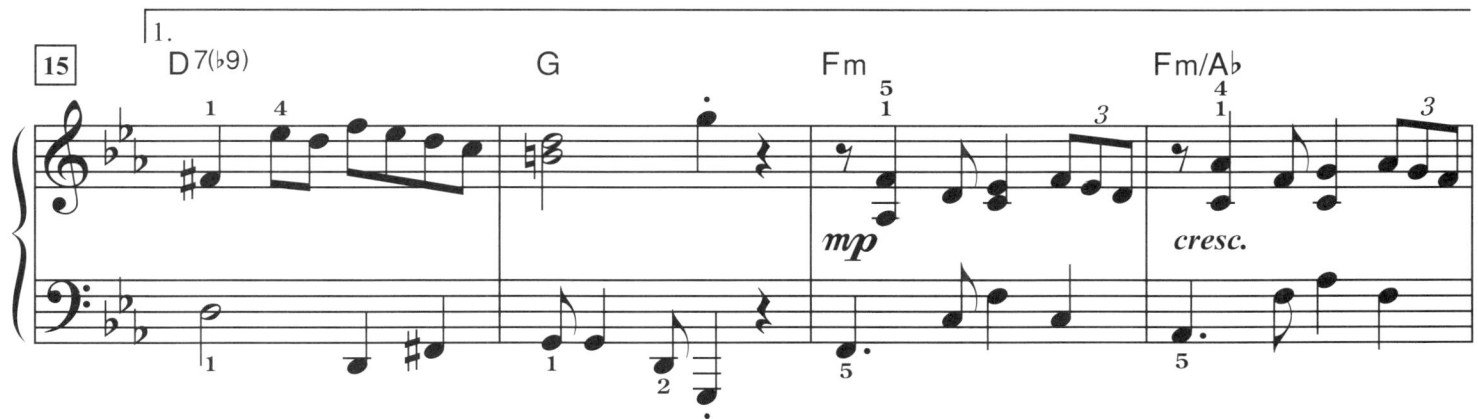
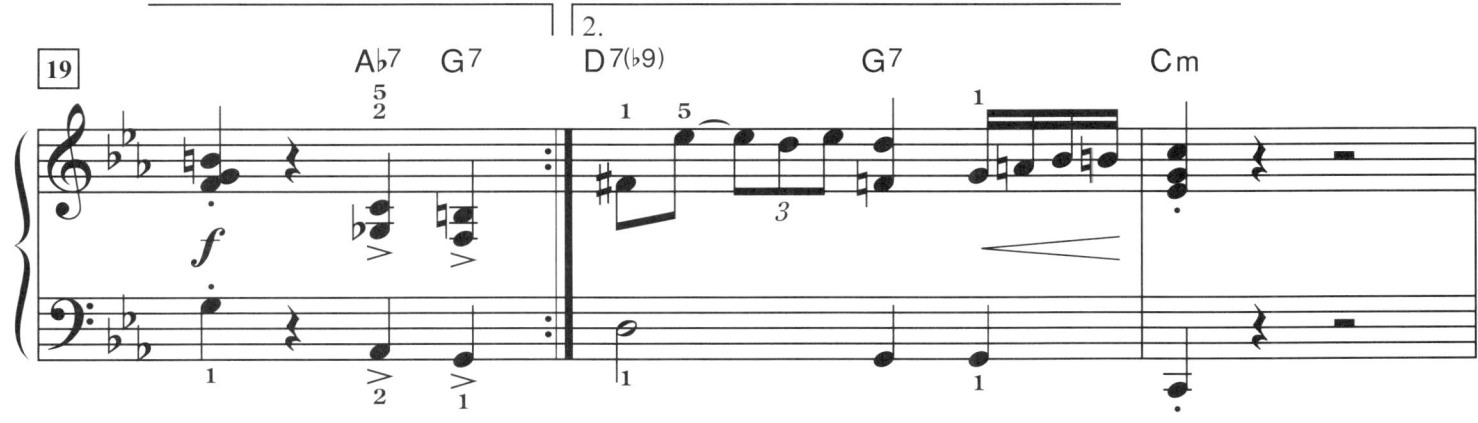

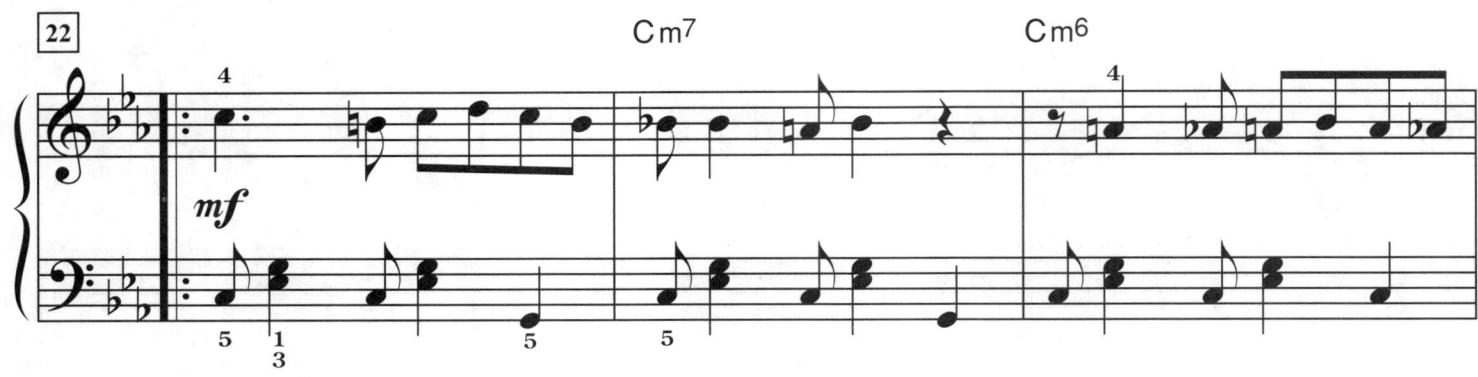
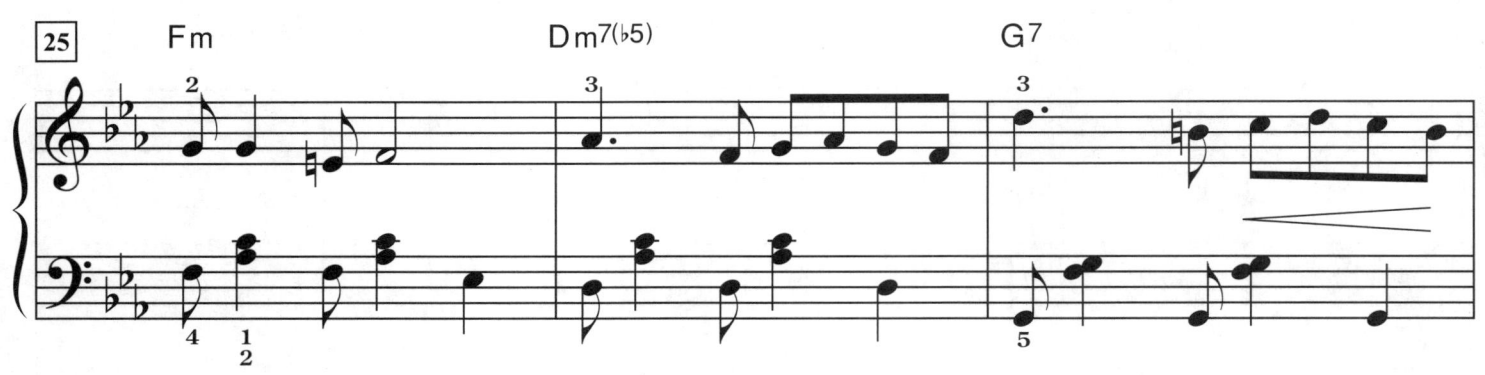
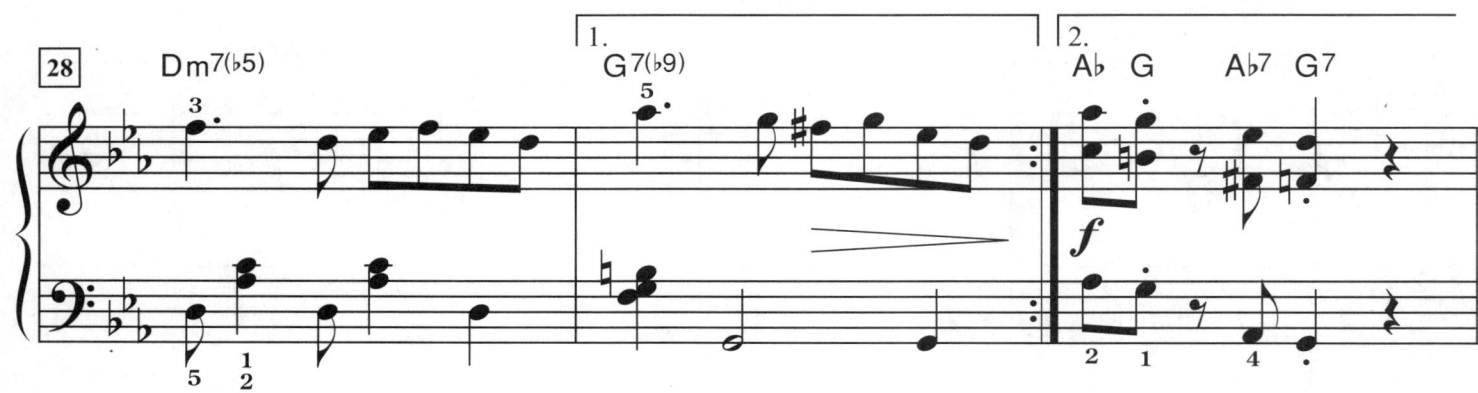

THE MUSIC OF CIRQUE DU SOLEIL®

"O™" MYSTÈRE™ LIVE SALTIMBANCO™ DRALION™ LE BEST OF

    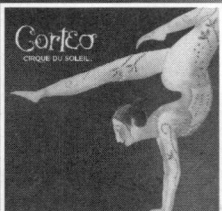

ALEGRÌA™ QUIDAM™ LA NOUBA™ VAREKAI™ CORTEO™

ZUMANITY™ SOLARIUM-DELIRIUM REMIX KÀ™ DELIRIUM KOOZA™

NOW AVAILABLE ON CD!

CIRQUEDUSOLEIL.COM